BRITISH STEAM ENGINES

The Memorabilia Collection

igloobooks
.com

Published in 2012
by Igloo Books Ltd
Cottage Farm
Sywell
NN6 0BJ
www.igloobooks.com

Images supplied courtesy of Getty Images.

SHE001 0812
2 4 6 8 10 9 7 5 3 1
ISBN 978-0-85780-778-6

Distributed in association with G2 Entertainment Limited
Printed and manufactured in China

Contents

Part One	**Introduction**	6-7
Chapter One	**Early Pioneers**	10-13
Chapter Two	**Steam Goes Public**	14-15
Chapter Three	**The Rainhill Trials**	16-23
Chapter Four	**Robert Stephenson & Co.**	24-29
Chapter Five	**Alternative Practices**	30-33
Chapter Six	**Steam Abroad**	34-37
Chapter Seven	**Further Developments**	38-45
Chapter Eight	**Competition in the South**	46-49
Chapter Nine	**Railway Rivalry**	50-55
Chapter Ten	**Standardisation & Imported Technology**	56-61
Chapter Eleven	**Grouping**	62-69
Chapter Twelve	**World War II**	70-71
Chapter Thirteen	**Nationalisation & BR Standard Locomotives**	72-81
Chapter Fourteen	**Steam in Decline 1954 to 1968**	82-93
Chapter Fifteen	**Epilogue**	94-95
Part Two	**Three Famous Men of Steam**	96-99
Chapter Sixteen	**George Stephenson Visionary**	100-129
Chapter Seventeen	**Robert Stephenson Grand Overseer**	130-143
Chapter Eighteen	**Brunel the Heroic Engineer**	144-159

Part One
Introduction

Twenty-one years after Trevithick had first demonstrated that self-propelled steam engines could haul colliery wagons better than horses, the first public railway, the Stockton and Darlington, commenced operation. A machine which resembled a large iron grasshopper on wheels attracted the awe and attention of the local populace. Like the horses that still laboured in the service of Mankind the strange machine had a body heat that could be felt as the onlookers approached with wary steps. It smelled of hot iron and warm oil and above its tall chimney the air shimmered, enlivened by the rising gases from its furnace. Its attendant driver and grimy fireman performed arcane and unfamiliar acts standing aloof from the crowd on the small footplating fixed to the machine's barrel, and lo, the machine's metal limbs twitched and its breath came in gasps as it lurched into movement. With no horse in the shafts and dripping water that fizzed and spat at the flinching yet delighted audience, it slowly rolled forward, creaking, squeaking, its iron wheels bearing down on iron rails.

A hundred and eighty years later the driver of any steam locomotive will find himself and his machine to be the object of intense interest. Delight will shine in the eyes of young children as they mimic with their arms the rise and fall of the coupling rods, or whoop in imitation of the engine's whistle as it runs into the station. Quite clearly this machine has enduring charisma. We who are privileged to operate them are no less entranced by the need to learn and practice the art of managing their power, and are no less aware of the beauty of their varied shapes and distinctive 'voices'.

Today when most of us find that computers have taken the satisfaction out of performing almost all jobs, be they administrative or manual, eight hundred people a year ask me to teach them to drive a steam engine. Men (and women) of all ages and from around the world have applied themselves to the hard and dirty work of managing a steam locomotive to a safe and efficient standard under close supervision. In some cases an introductory session sets them off on the long (ten-year) road to qualifying as a driver on a preserved line. For the majority a one-day session fulfils a dream that was unrealised but ever present since childhood.

Although this book starts out with the large stationary pumping engines of Newcomen and Watt its main topic will be the railway steam locomotives that were made possible by the raising of working pressures and consequent miniaturisation of engines (a locomotive has at least two 'engines'). Locomotive is a long and sometimes cumbersome word, so I will often refer to them as engines instead. Today it is common for the public to ask

happens to be a professional operator of the machine in question and has done so for the major part of his adult life. This old engineman had a 'revelation' the other day when he stood on the footplate of the re-created broad gauge engine Firefly at the Didcot Railway Centre. I was in the company of driver Peter Jennings and fireman, and chairman of the Firefly group, Sam Bee. The revelation went like this: I was standing on the footplate of a small 2-2-2 tender locomotive, the size of the single driving wheel was about seven feet. Its splasher had openings through which the wheel spokes were visible and I was prevented from falling off the footplate by low ornamental railings, much like those that can sometimes be found surrounding a bed of flowers, and I was reminded of an early paddle steamer. In front of me I found no spectacle plate, no windows through which to look and hence no cab or cab roof! And yet Sam informed me that this class of locomotive regularly ran trains to Paddington from Westbury at speeds of up to sixty miles per hour, in all weathers and by night and day.

me which 'train' they will drive when they mean which engine. I suppose the multiple unit diesel or electric sets that make up the modern train may have blurred the distinction between the conveyance and the power source for the average passenger.

This study, of the development of the steam locomotive over a two hundred year period will explain 'why engines look the way they do'. It will offer a general description of the way they work and of how the men that developed them came together then branched out on their individual paths of creative effort.

The overall 'dish' will be flavoured by the 'spice' that is unavoidable if the 'cook'

Now, I know what this means, because I have driven old tender locomotives in reverse at almost the same speed. In the winter it is horrible and painful to the ears, the eyes and the jaw! And we had a cab and cab roof around us. For the first time I saluted the courage and strength of the men that did their work with less than a garden gate between them and being cast overboard at speed. Between them and the elements that struck at them from all sides while one shovelled and the other peered, watery eyed, looking for dim oil lamps that signalled yay or nay to their onward rush.

Introduction

And the brakes were yet to be made perfect, and they did eighteen-hour days very often because "one man one engine" was the rule and they would have hated another man's hand to operate 'their' engine.

So for the first time I appreciated the courage of these old timers who were the 'astronauts' of their age. Now the early history of the steam engine came to life and I looked anew at the old prints and plans of Stephenson's, Gooch's and Crampton's machines. Dry historical facts are enlivened. The early days, made tedious by endless repetition in text books, are, to this engine-driving man at least, now full of human endeavour and stoicism. As the story unfolds we must imagine these 'old timers' regaling newcomers to their craft with tales of derring-do (we still do this to newcomers to the footplate). The hours on duty had to be reduced before the sleep inducing over all cabs could be introduced in Britain. Improvements in steel led to faster speeds. Improvements to pay led to larger engines, therefore higher productivity from less engines per train and less engine crews to work them.

Enginemen were seldom as scruffy as the average film director or costume manager dictates to the professional 'stunt driver' of steam locomotives today! Please note... enginemen were generally the dandies of the manual workers, "silk hatted aristocrats of the line" wrote someone. Main line drivers and firemen wore collars and ties. Drivers had polished shoes. Overalls were sometimes starched by mother at home. One has only to look at the old prints of enginemen and early photographs to see the pride taken in the turnout of the locomotive and its crew.

The locomotives of Britain were exported and adapted to the rougher conditions prevailing in the USA and elsewhere. Many of the adaptations came back to the home country and carried forward the improvements into British practice. Particularly in the case of the GWR which became American/French in order to create the best boiler and engine layout of the day.

Experimental designs are hard to justify to those that have to pay for them and perhaps lose the prospect of dividends if a mistake is made by the Chief Mechanical Engineer. Following America's lead, simplicity of maintenance and cheapness of construction eventually became the order of the day in the final sad days of main line British steam.

But, as in all good stories, the hero - defeated, succumbs only to bound back reinvigorated - in our case by the undiminished desire of laymen and some stubborn railwaymen to see and operate their beloved steam locomotives again. We have today several hundred examples of the old machines still operating, with a small number of completely new machines outshopped or in progress.

When you read this account of the history of steam you will find many omissions from the full story. Please forgive me. In compensation I have given an insider's view that may help you to understand the human side of those events. Throughout my research and throughout my career one wonderful fact keeps emerging: the love that Mankind had and still has for this machine. From the cleaner to the shedmaster. The spotter to the railway doyen. The apprentice to the Chief Mechanical Engineer. The history of steam is also the history of those who spent their lives in its thrall. It is a familiar yet inspiring story we offer in this book.

Chapter One

Early Pioneers

By the end of the eighteenth century the creations of Newcomen and Watt had brought to light the power available for the use of Mankind by the harnessing of steam. Some two hundred and fifty years later we in our nuclear age may easily forget that the power we rely on today still depends on water turned into steam, which is then used to make electricity. Miniaturisation may be a modern buzzword but this is essentially what first William Murdoch and later Richard Trevithick achieved just before the turn of the nineteenth century. They discovered that engines could be made much smaller if the pressure of the steam used to drive them was increased, and it eventually occurred to both men that it might be possible to put such an engine onto wheels. In 1784 Murdoch built a three wheeled model powered by a spirit lamp that he tested one Sunday evening near his home at Redruth. The little model hissed and spat furiously as it twisted and turned about, its trial run successful enough to be the source of some consternation to the local congregation, many of whom were convinced they were being confronted by a manifestation of the devil as they left the church. Trevithick made a full size road vehicle in 1802 and, together with his assistant Andrew Vivian, drove it from Redruth to Plymouth, then shipped it to London for further demonstration. After suffering a couple of setbacks he lost interest in the project and turned to rail mounted engines. Two years later at Pen-y-darren in South Wales, he produced a travelling engine that was to be the world's first steam railway locomotive. The engine was notable for the fact that it ran on smooth flangeless wheels within smooth flanged iron plates demonstrating that given sufficient weight the wheels would maintain their grip under power. Unfortunately however, this weight was too much for the iron plates designed for horse-drawn traffic, and many of them broke under the strain. Despite this hazard, Trevithick's engine hauled a ten ton load more than nine miles, the journey taking four hours to complete. As the engine had only one piston it would have been necessary to push or lever it into motion should the piston have stopped at either extremity of its travel. Also, as there was no means of admitting water to the boiler the entire run had to be completed on a single filling - fortunately the steam pressure was low.

The advantage of making smooth surfaces over which to run horse-drawn wagons had been discovered in antiquity. Instead of creating full blown Roman road surfaces a couple of strips of hard wood were found to be sufficient to ease the passage of wheels over soft ground, and the continuation of this process lead to the creation of 'plateways'. At Pen-y-darren these wooden plateways had been replaced by flanged iron plates in common with many colliery railways at the time. When it was later found that the flanged plates collected rubbish they were discarded in favour of edge rails on which flanged wheels could run and take guidance on curves with minimal friction. Gradients too steep for horses were surmounted by rope haulage from fixed engine houses. For the really steep gradients at the Middleton Colliery owned by John Blenkinsop, Leeds engineer Matthew Murray in 1812 built a steam engine driven by a toothed wheel engaging in a rack cast integrally with the rails. The engine was constructed with minimum weight, and thus minimal adhesion, to avoid the problems with the

brittle iron plateway. The rack gear provided the locomotive with the traction necessary to climb the colliery gradients. In order to make an engine that would start on a hill without needing to be pushed or levered into action, Murray fitted not one but two steam cylinders and set one crank at ninety degrees to the other, thus avoiding 'centring' on a dead spot. A year later at Wylam Colliery, William Hedley demonstrated that a rack was unnecessary when by experimentation he discovered the precise amount of adhesive weight needed for a given load. His engine had a 'U' shaped flue tube that ran most of the length of the boiler, the chimney being the same end of the boiler as the fire grate, thus providing the boiler with a larger heating surface. The exhaust pipe from the cylinders was inserted into the chimney stack, softening the harshness of the blast (which had frightened horses) and the engine became known as 'Puffing Billy'. However, Hedley had still not solved the problem of the fragile plateways, and eventually Puffing Billy's unsprung weight proved to be such a nuisance that for a time the engine was converted to run on eight wheels to spread the load. Later the plateway was taken up and replaced by rails which were more able to support the weight of the engine, and in 1830 Puffing Billy was reconverted to her original four wheel configuration. Subsequently this engine worked on the Wylam Colliery until 1862 when a change of gauge finally forced her retirement. However, Puffing Billy was preserved and can still be seen today on display in the London Science Museum.

None of the engines described so far had springs. This was because engines with vertical cylinders or which were driven by gears had to maintain a fixed relationship between axle centre and boiler centre. Any springing would cause disengagement of gearing or alter the clearances of the piston and cylinder end covers.

At Killingworth Colliery enginewright George Stephenson was earning himself a good reputation as a 'fixer' of sick engines. His father had been an engineman at the mine and at an early age George had taken a great interest in the pumping engines and the way they were made. His cleverness at engine 'doctoring' later made him famous and wealthy enough to provide his own son Robert with an excellent education that he himself had never had. The success of Hedley's engine at nearby Wylam Colliery prompted George's employers to ask him to build a similar engine for Killingworth. After some study of Hedley's engine, George began to construct a version with his own improvements to the valve gear, and with the two cylinders half set into the boiler barrel. This engine was completed in 1814. As in Hedley's engine the power was transmitted by gear wheels which ensured the cranks remained at right angles to each other. When the gears became worn out, George was instructed to build a second engine and this time he attached the connecting rods directly to the crank pins on the wheels. In order to prevent one wheelset slipping and altering the ninety degree setting the wheelsets were coupled together by rods between the frames fitted to cranked axles. However, the cranked axles were weak and the next engine Stephenson built in 1816 had a cog on each axle connected by a continuous chain which served to maintain the ninety degree relationship without weakening the axle. This engine was also fitted with steam springing. In both

BELOW
George Stephenson refined the Puffing Billy concept for Killingworth Colliery.

engines the exhaust steam was passed into the chimney, and their wheels were flanged. A further six engines of a similar type were built by George Stephenson between 1816 and 1822 before he began work on Locomotion.

The engines so far described were all working in the enclosed confines of the colliery for which they were built, they were not used for public haulage.

Chapter Two

Steam Goes Public

The success enjoyed by Stephenson's engines while shifting coal became widely known and Stephenson was soon asked by other colliery owners to build engines for them. In 1822 he completed an 8 mile line from the Hetton Colliery near Sunderland to the docks on the banks of the Wear. The steeper gradients of this line were worked by stationary engines and cables, but the more level sections were worked by steam locomotives built by himself to a design similar to the engines in use at Killingworth, with the chain coupled wheels. This experience was no doubt of great benefit to Stephenson when he became involved in a far more ambitious project. Incorporated by Act of Parliament in 1821, the Stockton and Darlington Railway was a public company, financed by public investors with the aim of building a public railway from the Durham coal fields around Darlington to the important port of Stockton-on-Tees. It was initially proposed that all traffic would be horse-drawn, but one of the major stockholders, a Quaker named Edward Pease, was persuaded by Stephenson that the freight traffic at least should be hauled by steam locomotives. Eventually after some wrangling, Stephenson was assigned the post of engineer, responsible for building the line and providing the steam locomotives to work the freight traffic. This appointment

LEFT
George Stephenson's first successful steam engine, the property of Hetton Colliery, takes part in the 1925 centenary procession celebrating the opening of the Stockton and Darlington.

was to prove more costly to the board of the S & D than they had originally anticipated. The first thing Stephenson stipulated was that he did not want to use the brittle cast iron fishbelly plates normally used on the colliery plateways. Wrought or rolled iron rails such as those patented by John Birkinshaw of the Bedlington Iron Works in 1820 were far more durable and were easily able to support the weight of any present or future locomotive that Stephenson might build to work the railway. Unfortunately they were also double the cost, but with a little persuasion and with the backing of Edward Pease, Stephenson eventually got his way. He also secured an order for three locomotives to work the line. Stephenson had initially decided to build the Stockton and Darlington Railway to a gauge of four feet eight inches, but he soon discovered that an extra half inch distance between the rails did much to reduce friction with-out any detriment to the security of the locomotives and rolling stock. 'Standard gauge' was born.

On Tuesday, 27th September 1825 the Stockton and Darlington Railway opened for business, the inaugural train being hauled by engine No.1, Locomotion, the first of the three steam locomotives George Stephenson had contracted to build for the new railway. Despite the fact that it had been agreed that all passenger traffic would be horse-drawn, a passenger coach of sorts had been built and was sandwiched in the middle of the train of more than thirty wagons of coal. Important dignitaries sat in the coach while every one else scrambled for any place they could get onto each of the coal wagons. Eventually everyone was in place and Locomotion began to wheeze her way forward. She succeeded in hauling the ninety ton train the length

of the line at a reasonably constant speed of between twelve and fifteen miles per hour, much to the satisfaction of all on board. Especially to the dignitaries in the coach, who for the very first time began to see that there might be some possibility of a return on their investments. In fact the railway was so successful that by the end of November the cost of transporting coal had been so reduced that the price of coal in Stockton had fallen by a third, eighteen months later it had been halved and the railway was already beginning to return a profit.

Locomotion was the first locomotive to be built in the new workshops of Robert Stephenson and Co. At around 8 tons in weight, she had a single flue boiler with a working pressure of 25 lb psi and two vertical cylinders each driving a pair of cast iron wheels four feet in diameter. The cylinders were connected directly to the driving wheels which were coupled either side of the engine with horizontal rods. The cranks were set ninety degrees to each other so that each cylinder was set to give its maximum output in turn with the other, thus minimising starting problems and enabling the engine to haul a train at a constant rate. The design was well suited for slow and heavy work, such as hauling many wagons of coal, but was inadequate for travel at any constant speed above 16 mph. Due to the single flue boiler the engine would simply run out of steam if too much was asked of it. However, George and Robert Stephenson were well aware of Locomotion's shortcomings and although they built three more like her for the coal trains of the Stockton and Darlington, they had something else in mind for faster trains of the future.

Chapter Three

The Rainhill Trials

The Stockton and Darlington was an unqualified success. Although all passenger traffic was initially drawn by horses, it was not long before someone had the idea of running mixed trains which were inevitably followed by passenger only trains hauled by faster engines. Not everybody was happy with this situation, however, and when George Stephenson declared that he could build an engine capable of a constant speed of twenty miles per hour a horrified member of the public wrote to the Quarterly Review: "What can be palpably more absurd and ridiculous, than the prospect held out of locomotives travelling twice as fast as stagecoaches? We would as soon expect the people of Woolwich to suffer themselves to be fired off in one of Congreve's ricochet-rockets, as trust themselves to the mercy of such a machine going at such a rate." No doubt reports from recent wars were fresh in the author's mind, the highly dangerous but very effective rockets designed by Sir William Congreve in 1805 and used by the British against both the French and the Americans having made a name for themselves in a typically spectacular fashion. As a matter of interest, George Stephenson had himself been drafted to fight in the Napoleonic wars but he paid another man to go in his place. It is fortunate indeed that he did so, otherwise it would have been many years before he could have returned to England to continue with his development of the steam engine - and he might well have been killed.

For some time it had been proposed to build a railway connecting the cities of Liverpool and Manchester and, despite the best efforts of landowners, horse breeders and coachmen, the necessary bill was eventually passed through Parliament. George Stephenson was appointed constructing engineer responsible for the survey, design

RIGHT
English railway engineer George Stephenson's locomotive 'Rocket' wins the reliability trials held at Rainhill Bridge, 1829.

BELOW
Critics compared the thought of riding at 20 mph to being fired from one of Sir William Congreve's rockets!

and execution of the civil engineering works required to build the railway. This entailed several particularly difficult works to overcome various natural features including a 'floating' embankment across Chat Moss, twelve square miles of peat bog, a two mile cutting at Olive Mount, a one and a half mile tunnel from Liverpool Station to Edgehill and the nine arch Sankey Viaduct. Naturally Stephenson was insistent that the line should be worked by steam engines, but the Liverpool and Manchester board of directors were not so sure. Many were still in favour of the more traditional methods of traction, either by horses or by cables powered by stationary engines. Fortunately this last option was projected to be extremely expensive, as it had been calculated that some twenty-one stationary steam engines would have been required to work the traffic the full length of the line. After

much lengthy and sometimes acrimonious debate the board eventually agreed to give the 'travelling engine' a chance. It was decided that a prize of £500 would be awarded to the best engine built within certain specifications, that ran economically and performed well according to certain set parameters as defined by the board.

George Stephenson had by now left the design and building of locomotive engines to his son, Robert, and his company Robert Stephenson and Co. His last effort had been the aptly named Experiment, an engine which he built in 1827 for the Stockton and Darlington Railway, and which had two flues in the boiler thus doubling the overall heating surface. Although the idea was later abandoned as boiler maintenance proved to be too complicated, Experiment had proved the benefits of the increased heating area. In 1828 Robert Stephenson

1829.

GRAND COMPETITION

OF

LOCOMOTIVES

ON THE

LIVERPOOL & MANCHESTER RAILWAY.

STIPULATIONS & CONDITIONS

On which the Directors of the Liverpool and Manchester Railway offer a Premium of £500 for the most Improved Locomotive Engine.

I.

The said Engine must "effectually consume its own smoke," according to the provisions of the Railway Act, 7th Geo. IV.

II.

The Engine, if it weighs Six Tons, must be capable of drawing after it, day by day, on a well-constructed Railway, on a level plane, a Train of Carriages of the gross weight of Twenty Tons, including the Tender and Water Tank, at the rate of Ten Miles per Hour, with a pressure of steam in the boiler not exceeding Fifty Pounds on the square inch.

III.

There must be Two Safety Valves, one of which must be completely out of the reach or control of the Engine-man, and neither of which must be fastened down while the Engine is working.

IV.

The Engine and Boiler must be supported on Springs, and rest on Six Wheels; and the height from the ground to the top of the Chimney must not exceed Fifteen Feet.

V.

The weight of the Machine, WITH ITS COMPLEMENT OF WATER in the Boiler, must, at most, not exceed Six Tons, and a Machine of less weight will be preferred if it draw AFTER it a PROPORTIONATE weight; and if the weight of the Engine, &c., do not exceed FIVE TONS, then the gross weight to be drawn need not exceed Fifteen Tons; and in that proportion for Machines of still smaller weight—provided that the Engine, &c., shall still be on six wheels, unless the weight (as above) be reduced to Four Tons and a Half, or under, in which case the Boiler, &c., may be placed on four wheels. And the Company shall be at liberty to put the Boiler, Fire Tube, Cylinders, &c., to the test of a pressure of water not exceeding 150 Pounds per square inch, without being answerable for any damage the Machine may receive in consequence.

VI.

There must be a Mercurial Gauge affixed to the Machine, with Index Rod, showing the Steam Pressure above 45 Pounds per square inch; and constructed to blow out a Pressure of 60 Pounds per inch.

VII.

The Engine to be delivered complete for trial, at the Liverpool end of the Railway, not later than the 1st of October next.

VIII.

The price of the Engine which may be accepted, not to exceed £550, delivered on the Railway; and any Engine not approved to be taken back by the Owner.

N.B.—The Railway Company will provide the ENGINE TENDER with a supply of Water and Fuel, for the experiment. The distance within the Rails is four feet eight inches and a half.

THE LOCOMOTIVE STEAM ENGINES,

WHICH COMPETED FOR THE PRIZE OF £500 OFFERED BY THE DIRECTORS OF THE LIVERPOOL AND MANCHESTER RAILWAY COMPANY.

DRAWN TO A SCALE ⅛ INCH TO A FOOT.

THE "ROCKET" OF MR. ROBT. STEPHENSON OF NEWCASTLE,

WHICH DRAWING A LOAD EQUIVALENT TO THREE TIMES ITS WEIGHT TRAVELLED AT THE RATE OF 12½ MILES AN HOUR, AND WITH A CARRIAGE & PASSENGERS AT THE RATE OF 24 MILES. COST PER MILE FOR FUEL ABOUT THREE HALFPENCE.

THE "NOVELTY" OF MESSRS. BRAITHWAITE & ERRICSSON OF LONDON,

WHICH DRAWING A LOAD EQUIVALENT TO THREE TIMES ITS WEIGHT TRAVELLED AT THE RATE OF 20¾ MILES AN HOUR, AND WITH A CARRIAGE & PASSENGERS AT THE RATE OF 32 MILES. COST PER MILE FOR FUEL ABOUT ONE HALFPENNY.

THE "SANSPAREIL" OF MR. HACKWORTH OF DARLINGTON,

WHICH DRAWING A LOAD EQUIVALENT TO THREE TIMES ITS WEIGHT TRAVELLED AT THE RATE OF 15 MILES AN HOUR. COST FOR FUEL PER MILE ABOUT TWO PENCE.

The Rainhill Trials

built a four wheeled engine called Lancashire Witch for the Bolton and Leigh Railway. Instead of the normal vertical cylinders, this engine was the first to have her cylinders inclined and mounted at the rear of the boiler, directly driving the front two wheels. This arrangement allowed the axles of the locomotive to be properly sprung for the first time. The locomotive Robert Stephenson built for the Rainhill Trials was the

culmination of these designs but had one very important additional feature. As the result of a suggestion by Henry Booth, the secretary of the Liverpool and Manchester Railway, the engine was built with a boiler incorporating

twenty-five three-inch copper tubes which considerably increased its heating capacity. At six feet long and with a working pressure of 50 lbs psi, the boiler was the first to have a proper firebox at the rear. The inclined cylinders were mounted either side of the firebox and drove the front pair of single driving wheels directly via connecting rod and crankpin. The exhaust from each cylinder was directed up the chimney via blast pipes carefully tapered to provide the optimum draw on the fire. The entire locomotive weighed less than four and a half tons, not an awful lot more than the tender that was attached to it which weighed over three tons when fully laden with water and coal. The engine proved to be capable of sustained speeds of up to thirty miles an hour and was duly christened Rocket, partly, no doubt, as a tribute to her fleet-footedness, but possibly also as an unabashed gesture to all those who doubted that such a machine was either safe or desirable.

There were many prospective entries to the Liverpool and Manchester's contest, some less sensible than others. These were gradually weeded out until eventually there were only four contenders for the prize other than Rocket. One was a four wheeled locomotive named Sanspareil entered by Timothy Hackworth, another was the appropriately named Novelty, a highly unusual four wheeled engine entered by John Braithwaite and Captain John Ericsson, a Swede. A third engine named Perseverance, also had four wheels and was the entry of a Scot named Timothy Burstall. The only other suitable contestant was Edward Bury of Liverpool, and although he was not able to complete his engine in time for the trials he was later to make significant contributions towards

The Rainhill Trials

the evolution of the steam engine.

Hackworth had previously worked for George Stephenson and at the time of the contest was the locomotive superintendent of the Stockton and Darlington Railway. He was noted for his rebuilding of an engine that had been given the disparaging nickname of 'Chittaprat' because of the terrible noise it made. Supplied by a Newcastle firm for the Stockton and Darlington Railway, No. 5 had four cylinders and four driving wheels, with a pair of cylinders each driving a separate pair of driving wheels without any coupling between the two. The engine had not been a success and when it was damaged in an accident, Hackworth took the opportunity to scrap it and make use of its boiler. The result was Royal George, a six coupled engine capable of hauling thirty-two wagons of coal weighing around a hundred and thirty tons at a constant speed of five miles an hour, and was at the time one of the most powerful locomotives ever built. Sanspareil was virtually a shortened four wheel version of Royal George, she had the same 'U' tube boiler and a pair of vertical cylinders mounted over the rear axle. However, she weighed more than five hundredweight over the stipulated maximum and was disqualified although she was later allowed to take part in the trials. By contrast Novelty, the engine of Braithwaite and Ericsson, seemed lightly built, almost elegant in appearance. She easily attained the fastest speed of all the contestants and was a great favourite with the crowd of spectators. Built with an ingenious combined vertical and horizontal boiler feeding a pair of vertical cylinders, Novelty was the only locomotive in the trials to carry her own coal and water supply and has since been regarded as the first

tank engine. Burstall's engine, Perseverance, had a vertical boiler mounted on a platform over two pairs of driving wheels, but she was unable to attain the required speed and was withdrawn from the contest.

The Rainhill Trials began on 8th October 1829, and were conducted over a seven day period on the Rainhill Level, a stretch of track less than two miles long near the Liverpool end of the Liverpool and Manchester Railway. A grandstand had been built at the mid point of the track and on the first day some 15,000 people turned up to watch the spectacle. Each contestant was required to complete two runs of thirty-seven and a half miles each, which represented a return trip of the length of the Liverpool and Manchester line. This meant that each engine had to make many journeys up and down the track while attached to a suitable load. One of the requirements made by the Liverpool and Manchester board was that each locomotive should "consume its own smoke", as they were anxious about the nuisance that might be created by engines belching thick black clouds of soot and ashes. At the trial each of the contestants burned coke to get around this problem. Both Rocket and Sanspareil used blast pipes that directed exhaust steam from the cylinders up the chimney to draw the fire. Sanspareil's blast pipe was a little severe and was prone to sending a large part of the contents of her fire-flue straight up her chimney, much to the consternation of anyone who happened to be standing nearby. Novelty's fire was drawn not by the exhaust blast but by a set of bellows which failed during one of her runs leaving the unfortunate engine unable to make steam. During the many journeys back and forth both Sanspareil and Novelty were beset by various problems until eventually Novelty's boiler failed, as did the boiler feed water pump on Sanspareil, leaving both engines unable to continue. Only Rocket met the board's stringent requirements including running reliably for the entire distance while hauling a load. The Stephensons were not only awarded the £500 prize, but also an order for a further seven locomotives similar to Rocket to work the Liverpool and Manchester Railway. It is interesting to note, however, that according to The Liverpool Mercury of October 1829 Rocket was an "old-fashioned locomotive engine" and that the engine entered by Messrs Braithwaite and Ericsson was a "decided improvement in the arrangement, the safety, simplicity, and the

smoothness and steadiness of a locomotive engine". The Mercury further reported that but for an unfortunate break down Novelty would have been a clear winner, and that it was the opinion of the general public and "nine-tenths of the engineers and scientific men now in Liverpool" that the principle and construction of all future locomotives would follow her design. Of course the real secret of Rocket's success was hidden from public view, her firebox and multi-tube boiler were a major breakthrough in locomotive design and the foundation of what would become standard practice in the construction of steam engines. Thus, the Stephensons' innovative design and superb workmanship had won the day at Rainhill, and had secured the future of steam traction on the railways.

RIGHT
John Braithwaite and Captain John Ericsson's Novelty was aptly named, for it was of a most unusual design.

Chapter Four
Robert Stephenson & Co.

The business of Robert Stephenson and Company was formed in 1823 by a partnership between George and Robert Stephenson and Edward Pease, the latter providing much of the financial backing. Land was purchased in Forth Street, Newcastle-on-Tyne and a factory built with the particular purpose of steam locomotive construction in mind. It was a bold move at the time because many people, including those who were later to become railway shareholders and board members, were not entirely convinced that steam was a good thing. There were landowners that did not want to see railways 'ruining' the countryside, coach proprietors and horse breeders who were concerned that their business might suffer, and there were those who thought that to travel at speeds in excess of twenty miles an hour was a sin against Nature, and that steam engines were just plain dangerous. If the dissenters had had their way the operating life of Robert Stephenson and Co. would have been extremely short.

The new company received its first order for two steam locomotives from the board of the Stockton and Darlington Railway in 1824 but only the first of them, Locomotion, had been completed by the time the Stockton and Darlington opened

in 1825. Robert Stephenson, though only twenty years of age, had in 1824 accepted a post with a mining company in South America, which is where he spent the next three years. George Stephenson found himself caught up in the almost manic desire for railways that had spread countrywide, and in 1824 he was consultant to no less than four separate railway companies, including the Liverpool and Manchester. Accordingly, the new locomotive works in Forth Street had become a little neglected and Edward Pease began to wonder at the wisdom of his investment. However, George carried on while Robert was abroad, and the orders were slowly fulfilled. He completed his last engine early in 1826, which was Experiment, built with two flues in the

boiler in an effort to increase the surface heating area. Once Robert returned from South America the locomotive building began in earnest. In 1827 Twin Sisters was completed, a peculiar engine built especially for hauling ballast trains while building the Liverpool and Manchester Railway. As she was expected to work over some temporarily steep inclines during the construction of the railway she had been built with two boilers. This was so that which ever way the incline one boiler flue was always covered with water, and the fire in the other was allowed to die down or go out.

Robert Stephenson and Co. built many further engines for collieries and the new

railways that had begun to spring up around the country, and in each of these engines there was some improvement, some refinement of the design as was seen with the Lancashire Witch built for the Bolton and Leigh Railway and then later on with Rocket. Winning the Rainhill trials was an obvious boost, as was the order for the further seven locomotives for the Liverpool and Manchester Railway. However, the company did not rest on its laurels and continued to experiment and improve the design of each subsequent locomotive built. Thus the later engines of the "Rocket" class were built with less steeply inclined cylinders to improve their stability and the last of these, Northumbria, was the first engine to be built with a smokebox. When the Liverpool and Manchester Railway opened on 15th September 1830, the unfortunate William Huskisson, MP for Liverpool, was accidentally knocked down by Rocket during the festivities. George Stephenson driving Northumbria raced the injured man to Eccles for medical attention. He covered the fifteen miles from Parkside, the scene of the accident, to Eccles in less than twenty-five minutes, an average speed of thirty-six miles an hour. No man had ever travelled so fast before. Unfortunately, however, the mercy dash was in vain, Huskisson's injuries were too severe and he died later that night.

Eighteen months after Rainhill Rocket was extensively modified. Her chimney was shortened and remounted on the boiler on a smokebox and the incline of her cylinders was reduced so they were nearly horizontal. Despite these refinements the pace of technology was such that by 1830 Rocket and her sisters were obsolete. She still continued to work the Liverpool and Manchester until 1836 when she was sold

to a colliery in Carlisle where she worked for a further three years. By then the engine was considered to be of insufficient power and too worn out to be of any further use, though fortunately she was not scrapped. In 1862 the colliery company presented the derelict remains to the Patent Office Museum, later the Science Museum, where she can still be seen today.

The next significant advance in the development of the steam locomotive was Planet, completed in October 1830 for the Liverpool and Manchester Railway. This four wheeled engine had her two cylinders placed inside the frame under the smokebox where the warmth prevented the cylinders cooling and condensing the steam, an idea

suggested to Stephenson by Trevithick some years before as a means of improving fuel economy. The rear wheels were driven via connecting rods to the double cranked rear axle. Two months later Mercury was completed, a sister engine in most respects except that the frames were raised above the level of the driving axle, and for freight-working further similar locomotives were built with the wheels coupled together. Such was the success of these engines that their fame spread far and wide and everybody wanted one. Robert Stephenson and Co. were soon swamped with orders, not only from developing railways in Britain but also those from many countries abroad who were all eager to take advantage of this new and revolutionary form of transport. Even so, there were still further improvements that could be made, as the "Planets" had proved to be unstable at speed, and their firebox capacity inadequate. Stephenson extended the locomotive frames behind the firebox and added a trailing axle to improve the stability of the engine and enable a bigger firebox to be used. Thus the "Patentee"

class of locomotive was created, and many of these engines were built. They were generally of the 2-2-2 wheel arrangement with two large driving wheels on the centre axle and outside frames. It was a versatile type, able to be optimised for either passenger or freight use, and many variations were built and exported for the countless fledgling railways under construction both in Britain and around the world.

Despite the success of the "Patentee" class, Robert Stephenson knew there was still room for further improvement. In 1842 he discovered that the chimneys and smokeboxes were beginning to burn out prematurely on many of his engines and, after some experimentation, discovered that the smokeboxes were reaching a temperature in excess of 700 degrees Fahrenheit. This was, of course, a terrible waste. No useful work was performed by a red hot smokebox. Stephenson's solution to this was his 'long boilered' locomotives, where the tubes and the boiler were lengthened by between four and five feet. He also gave the new engines a large square firebox with a dome on top

LEFT
Stephenson's 'long boiler' locomotives always suffered from pitching problems.

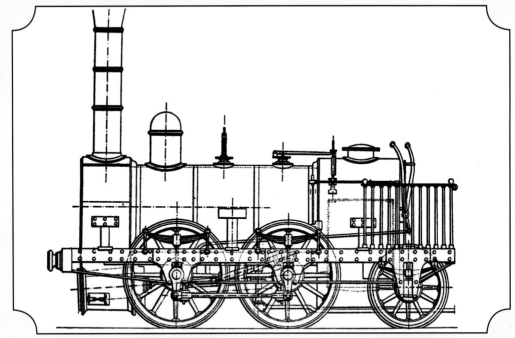

to collect steam for the outside cylinders. However, the three axles with the large centre driving wheel had to be crammed together under the boiler otherwise the engine would be unable to negotiate any but the most broadly radiused curves. This left the large firebox overhanging at one end and the smokebox and cylinders at the other, causing the locomotive to pitch back and forth if it began to travel at any speed. Despite a number of attempts to cure this problem by changing the wheel arrangement to 4-2-0 or even 4-2-2 with the addition of a trailing axle, the pitching motion was never completely eliminated. Because of this the 'long boiler' locomotive enjoyed limited success as a passenger hauling engine. However, as six coupled 0-6-0 engines the class were found to be very suitable for heavy goods traffic and many saw long service hauling coal trains on lines like the Stockton and Darlington where

freight was the mainstay of operation.

Another important advance to come out of the workshops of Robert Stephenson and Co. was what became known as 'Stephenson's link motion', though it was in fact developed by one of the company's fitters, William Howe, in 1842. This eliminated the reliability problems of the previously used fork or gab gear, and provided the engine driver with a means of 'cutting off' steam for expansive working.

George Stephenson died in 1848. The company he set up in 1823 with his son had made Robert Stephenson a millionaire by the time of his death in 1859. Robert Stephenson and Co. carried on building locomotives for almost another century, merging with Hawthorn Leslie and Co. in 1937. More importantly, the true legacy the Stephensons left behind was the foundation of a transport system that changed the lives of millions of people all over the world forever.

Chapter Five

Alternative Practices

Although pioneers, the Stephensons were far from being the only people building steam engines in those early years. Edward Bury of Liverpool, although unable to produce an engine in time for the trials at Rainhill, was an engineer of considerable skill. The engines he built were all four wheeled, either 2-2-0 or 0-4-0, and were distinctive in appearance with their inside bar frames and round dome-topped fireboxes usually finished in polished copper. Bury's engines were generally well designed and well built, and in the early years they

were quite able to manage the traffic of the time. However, they were small and light in weight, and as the trains they hauled became heavier they were less able to cope satisfactorily with the loads required of them. Edward Bury was locomotive superintendent of the London and Birmingham Railway and he succeeded in persuading the board that his own small locomotives were adequate and that to build larger ones would be an unnecessary expense. The consequence of this policy was that London and Birmingham trains would frequently be double headed and sometimes three or even four locomotives would be required to haul the train. Not a terribly efficient way to run a railway! However, Bury's engines had some important innovations, and the cheap, lightweight bar frames and domed-topped firebox found much favour with railway lines abroad, particularly in America.

In August 1835 a new railway company was incorporated to build a line connecting Bristol to London, and to build it the board selected a brilliant young engineer named Isambard Kingdom Brunel. In 1829 Brunel had impressed many of the board members with his design of a suspension bridge that won a competition to bridge the River Avon at Bristol, and he seemed a perfect choice to build their Great Western Railway despite his comparatively young age of 29. Brunel believed in speed, he

LEFT
Isambard Kingdom Brunel was chosen to build the railway between Bristol and London.

ABOVE
A steam train on the Birmingham Railway emerging from the Chalk Farm box tunnel in London, 1860.

thought that the travelling public would better appreciate a journey made as in as much comfort as possible and which was as short as possible. He immediately dismissed the four foot eight and a half inch gauge used by George Stephenson as being too narrow. He wanted to have engines with the widest firebox possible in order to produce the greatest amount of steam, and on the wider gauge coaches could be built with

a low centre of gravity and with increased space and comfort inside for the passengers. He decided on a gauge of seven feet and a quarter inch and engineered the line to be as straight as possible, ensuring that all curves were of the greatest possible radius. The first engines brought in to work the line were unsuccessful, and in 1837 he hired another young engineer named Daniel Gooch, then only 21, to acquire something more suitable. By a stroke of luck a couple of large "Patentee" type locomotives originally built for the five foot six inch gauge New Orleans Railway in America by Robert Stephenson and Co. had been returned unsold. They were modified for the seven foot and a quarter inch Great Western Railway and as North Star and Morning Star turned in some pretty impressive performances. The first section of the line from London to Maidenhead opened in 1838, and in that year North Star hauled a passenger train at an average speed of thirty-eight miles an hour while reaching a top speed of forty-five miles per hour. At the time this was sensational. All

Brunel's theories and advocacy of the broad gauge had been vindicated. By 1841 the line to Bristol had been completed and the Great Western Railway gradually began to extend its broad gauge northwards. An intense rivalry began between the broad gauge advocates and the supporters of Stephenson's standard gauge, claims and counter claims abounded. But it was the passenger who had to put up with the chaos at break of gauge stations. Eventually the government realised that it had to act, and in 1845 a Royal Commission was set up to investigate the problem. By this time Gooch was building Great Western engines in the GWR's own workshops at Swindon. In 1846 he built a large "Patentee" type of locomotive that made a run from London to Swindon at an average speed of over 59 miles per hour. A year later by enlarging the "Patentee" design still further and adding another leading axle he created the first of the "Iron Duke" class, a 4-2-2 broad gauge engine that in its time was unrivalled for its speed and power. However, it was all to no avail, the findings of the Royal Commission clearly stated that for the railways to be of full benefit to the travelling public and to the nation in general, the gauge must be of a standard width throughout the country. And, as at that time there was 1900 miles of four foot eight and a half inch track laid against only 274 miles of broad gauge, standard meant standard. In May 1892 the very last broad gauge train pulled out of Paddington Station, the GWR's London terminus, with suitable crowds lining the platforms to see her off. It must have been like saying goodbye to Concorde.

The success of the large fireboxed engines on Brunel's broad gauge prompted a number of experiments with standard gauge engines in order to achieve a similar effect. One of these was Stephenson's 'long boilered' engine with a wide firebox built behind the rear axle, another was a locomotive designed by Thomas Crampton, an engineer who had spent some time with Daniel Gooch on the Great Western. His idea was to have a deep firebox between the second and third axles with the large driving wheels mounted on the third axles, behind the firebox, giving the engine a 4-2-0 wheel arrangement. To avoid overly long connecting rods, the cylinders were brought back from the front of the engine and mounted between the first and second axles on the outside of the frames. This gave the engine the advantage of a large firebox but with good stability and none of the pitching motion experienced by 'long boilered' locomotives at high speed. In 1845 a Crampton locomotive reached a top speed of sixty-five miles per hour while hauling twelve coaches from London

to Wolverton on the London and North Western Railway. Despite this success, other designs superseded the Crampton in Britain although many were built on the Continent, particularly in France and in Germany.

Yet another variation of the "Patentee" type of locomotive was designed by David Joy in 1847 for the London, Brighton and South Coast Railway. Built by E B Wilson and Co. Jenny Lind had the usual "Patentee" style double frames but had her leading and trailing axles supported by the outside frame and the driving axle supported by the inside frame. With a boiler pressure of 120 lb psi, the highest known at the time, Jenny Lind ran at speeds in excess of fifty miles per hour during her first trials. She also proved to be remarkably stable due to the sideways play allowed to the leading pair of wheels by her construction. Such was the success of the locomotive that many more "Jenny Lind"s were built over a period of nearly forty years.

Chapter Six

Steam Abroad

Railway mania was not confined to the British Isles. With vast tracts of untamed country and enormous distances between major cities, America was quick to spot the advantages of the new form of transport. After some experimentation, the first commercial steam railway, the South Carolina Railroad, ran its first train on Christmas Day 1830. A train with over forty passengers on board was hauled by the brand new Best Friend of Charleston at speeds of up to twenty miles an hour. A few weeks later on 15th January 1831 the first regular train service was inaugurated and ran successfully for some months until June 1831 when Charleston's Best Friend suffered a boiler explosion.

In those early days many of the new railways that sprang up across America, purchased locomotives from Great Britain, very often from Robert Stephenson and Co. One of the better known of these imported engines was John Bull, a four wheeled "Planet" class engine that was sent in pieces to the Camden and Amboy Railroad in Pennsylvania in 1831. It was assembled by Isaac Dripps with a few modifications of his own, most notably a circular domed firebox and the very first 'pilot', a two wheeled leading bogie that assisted the locomotive in negotiating the tight curves of the lightly laid track. The 'pilot' also had a wedge shaped framework attached to the front of it designed to clear obstructions from the track before they derailed the locomotive. This device became known as a 'cowcatcher'. While standard gauge track was the most widely used throughout America (there were exceptions), the actual method of laying it was vastly different to the solid, precisely engineered permanent way as seen in the UK. With enormous distances to cover over rugged and often inhospitable country American engineers had to keep the costs down if they were to have a railway at all. Instead of bullhead rail being laid in chairs, flat bottomed rails were spiked directly to the sleepers. Instead of the superbly engineered lines with tunnels, viaducts and embankments designed to keep the track as level and straight as possible, in America the track was laid over whatever was deemed the most suitable route. Sharp curves and steep inclines could often not be avoided and the locomotives used had to be capable of negotiating these hazards. And, of course, most of the land was unfenced. Dripps's 'pilot' was soon seen to be a very useful idea and with a few modifications it rapidly became standard practice on all American railroads.

Generally, British engines were found to be unsuitable for the rough terrain of the New World, and the American locomotive industry rapidly became a home grown affair. Bury-style bar frames were almost universally

BELOW
An early American locomotive, The Sandusky made in Paterson, New Jersey worked on similar principles to its UK counterpart.

adopted as they were simple to build and suitably economic. For ease of maintenance all the moving parts and fittings were placed outside the frames where possible including the cylinders and connecting rods. Two pairs of coupled driving wheels were favoured as the resulting short wheel base enabled the locomotive to negotiate tight curves especially with the four wheel front bogie to guide it. A bell and a loud whistle were fitted to the engine in order to warn all creatures, four or two legged, of the locomotive's impending approach, and the cow-catcher took care of any that were too slow, too deaf or too stubborn. A powerful lamp was fitted to the front of the engine to provide further warning after dark. The loco-motives were built with comfortable and roomy cabs to protect the crew from the bitter winters and, as they were mostly fired with wood, they were fitted with large conical 'spark arresting' chimneys. This distillation of ideas became the standard American 4-4-0. Versatile, ubiquitous, many hundreds were built travelling many thousands of miles as they criss-crossed America, connecting the populations of each coast with the settlements of the interior. Variations of this type were in use for decades from the mid to late nineteenth century. Although the distances covered were vast the travelling speeds of the American trains were slow compared to the speed of trains in Britain and Europe. Frequent stops were required to refuel and water both the locomotive and the passengers, and long journeys must have been fairly tedious affairs. However, to anyone faced with a similar journey in a stagecoach, a steam train would have been an utter godsend, a true miracle of technology. Initially, railways in Europe tended to be built much like those in Britain. Standard

LEFT
A Union Pacific Rail Road locomotive in Utah with a 'cowcatcher' fixed to its front for removing cows that wander onto the railway line or to shunt fallen timber off the tracks.

gauge with rails set in chairs was the most usual type of track laid, and many of the first locomotives used on these lines were imported from Britain, often from Robert Stephenson and Co. Typical of these was the first steam engine to run in Germany, Adler, a small "Patentee" type that was exported from England, complete with an English driver, for the Nuremburg-Fürth Railway which opened in 1835. Robert Stephenson and Co. also licensed construction companies in other countries to build engines to their designs. The first engine to run in Belgium was a "Patentee" built locally under just such an arrangement and was called Le Belge. Italy's first engine was a "Patentee", as was the first engine to run on Russian metals on the St Petersburg to Pavlovsk railway opened in 1838. Another "Patentee" for Germany was built under license in Munich in 1841 by Joseph von Maffei, founder of a company that would become one of the leading locomotive manufacturers in Europe. Holland's first steam engines were two "Patentees" named Arend and Snelheid which worked the line from Amsterdam to Haarlem opened in 1839. A "Patentee" was the first locomotive to run on the inaugural five miles of track between Naples and Portici in the Kingdom of Naples. This engine was also built under license but by another Newcastle company, probably Robert Stephenson and Co. could not keep up with the demand.

France had her own pioneer, Marc Séguin, who in 1829, wholly independently of the Stephensons' work with Rocket, built a steam locomotive with a multi-tubular boiler to run on the line from St Etienne to Andrézieux. However, instead of using exhaust from the cylinders to draw the fire via a blast pipe in the chimney, he developed a complicated system of draughting using two large fans mounted on the tender and driven by belts from the trailing axle. The mechanics of this system proved to be unreliable and the engine was not a success as there was never sufficient draught on the fire. In France at this time the railways were generally regarded as little more than a mechanical oddity, and it was not until 1837 when the Péreire brothers opened the short line from Paris to St Germain that the French public began to realise what the rest of the world was on about. In 1842 the French government passed its Railway Law and from that time all railways were planned and built under strict government control. Among early locomotives used were the ubiquitous "Patentee" type, sometimes heavily modified. Later the Crampton style locomotive with single driving wheels mounted on the trailing axle proved popular, and many variations of these were seen on the lines running into and out of Paris.

As the years progressed, with experience and experimentation, most countries gradually developed their own locomotives and the means to construct them according to local conditions and requirements. However, the basic formula for every successful locomotive built can be traced back to Rocket, and the ingenuity of the Stephensons.

Chapter Seven
Further Developments

As the design of the steam locomotive improved and the railway system was extended throughout the country, more people began to travel further and faster than even before. With the introduction of dining cars and sleeping cars trains rapidly became heavier and heavier. To cope with these increasing loads bigger engines were built with ever larger fireboxes and boilers. The 2-2-2 locomotive with the single pair of driving wheels was still in general use for passenger work during the latter part of the nineteenth century, the design being enlarged and improved according to the requirements of the operating company. Many of the smaller lines slowly amalgamated to pool their resources and consolidate their respective shares of the market. In 1846 the Liverpool and Manchester joined with the London and Birmingham, the Manchester and Birmingham and the Grand Junction Railway to form the London and North Western Railway. The responsibilities for producing locomotive power for the LNWR was initially split between the Southern Division, based at Wolverton, and the Northern Division, based at Crewe. Each division had its own works and locomotive superintendent, and their philosophy and practice differed enormously. In charge of the Wolverton works was J E McConnell

who had previously been the superintendent of the Birmingham and Gloucester Railway based at Bromsgrove. In the year prior to the LNWR amalgamation he had designed and built a number of engines with inside frames and inside bearings, and these had been a great success. The first engines he built at Wolverton were an enlarged version of the BGR locomotives with large boilers and six foot six inch driving wheels. The high open splashers and the lack of an outside bearing to the driving wheels gave the engines a 'leggy' appearance, rapidly earning them the nickname 'Bloomers' after one Mrs Bloomer, a lady from America who was then championing the simplification of women's dress, including, horror of horrors, the wearing of trousers. Later versions of these engines had seven foot driving wheels, and in 1852 he designed a still larger locomotive with seven foot six driving wheels. At this time it was generally believed that engines should be built with the boiler positioned as low as possible within the frames to give as low a centre of gravity as possible and thus, so it was thought, better stability. The only problem with this philosophy was that the diameter of the driving wheels was necessarily restricted. McConnell disagreed with this theory; he believed that a high boilered engine was just as stable

BELOW
The West Coast
Express being
hauled by a
Bloomer locomotive
in 1865.

as long as it was properly constructed. The 'Bloomers' proved him right.

In complete contrast to the practice at Wolverton, the locomotive superintendent of the Northern Division of the LNWR at Crewe, Alexander Allan, favoured small locomotives. Some years before, The Grand Junction Railway had had several "Patentee" locomotives which had suffered broken crank axles. Allan had overcome this problem by rebuilding the engines with outside cylinders, creating what became known as the 'Crewe' type of locomotive. In common with Edward Bury, Allan believed that small engines were cheaper to build and to operate than large engines - which was true up to a point. As train loads became heavier more power was required to haul them, and for the Northern Division of the LNWR this meant that it was necessary to couple two, three, or sometimes even four engines together to haul one train. Any savings made by building small locomotives were more than expended in

the cost of the manpower required to drive and service them. Nonetheless, the 'Crewe' type of engine proved to be successful and reliable and nearly four hundred of them were built between 1845 and 1858, about a third of these being 2-2-2 types for passenger trains and the rest built as 2-4-0s for hauling freight. The livery of the Northern Division was a dark green colour, and passengers who had travelled up from London behind the large bright red Southern Division engines with their huge driving wheels must have wondered if they were still travelling with the same company when they saw the small green engines that were to take them on the Manchester.

The LNWR dubbed themselves the 'Premier Line' and in their publicity campaigns their London terminus at Euston was much touted as being the 'Gateway to the North'. It was therefore a source of great annoyance to the LNWR directors that the publicity machine of the Great Western

Further Developments

ABOVE
A GWR 4-2-2 broad gauge locomotive at Swindon Station in Wiltshire mid 1800s.

Railway was claiming faster and faster speeds for their express trains, especially as the famed broad gauge lines were gradually creeping ever northwards. They commissioned the Crewe works of the Northern Division to build three experimental express locomotives with the idea of proving to themselves and to the travelling public that standard gauge engines were just as good as anything running on the broad gauge. The three locomotives were completed in 1847. One was Courier, a Crampton with seven foot driving wheels mounted behind the firebox, another was Velocipede, designed by Alexander Allan, who thought that the very idea of the 'contest' was absurd and so did no more than build an enlarged version of his usual design with seven foot driving wheels. The third engine was designed by the Locomotive Superintendent of the Northern Division,

Francis Trevithick (son of Richard), who conversely to Allan thought it was vitally important not only to equal but to surpass the performance of the Great Western engines. Accordingly he designed a locomotive with eight foot six inch driving wheels, the largest to run on standard gauge track. As it was still considered desirable for an engine to have a low centre of gravity at the time, the boiler was placed underneath the driving axle with outside cylinders providing the motive force. The locomotive was named Cornwall, and she proved to be a success from her very first trial run as she reached the speed of seventy-nine miles per hour, one mile an hour faster than the speeds claimed by the Great Western engine. Cornwall was exhibited at the Great Exhibition of 1851 where she attracted a great deal of interest. In later years she was rebuilt by

John Ramsbottom with the boiler placed above the driving axle, and in this condition she gave many years of useful service hauling express trains between Liverpool and Manchester. Towards the end of the nineteenth century some fifty years later Cornwall was still considered to be one of the fastest engines in service provided she was not overloaded. One of the first locomotives to be deliberately earmarked for preservation, Cornwall can be seen today in the collection of the National Railway Museum at York.

In 1857 John Ramsbottom succeeded Trevithick as chief mechanical engineer of the Northern Division of the London and North Western Railway. His first express engine was a 2-2-2 'single' with driving wheels of seven feet seven and a half inches and the unprepossessing name Problem. Two important innovations helped to make the class one of the outstanding performers of its time. They were the first engines to be fitted with steam driven injectors to refill the boiler instead of the feed water pump that had been the only device previously available. The injector was the invention of a Frenchman named Henri Giffard, at the time more well known for his steam driven hydrogen(!) filled airships. The other advance was truly home grown, invented by Ramsbottom himself; the water trough. "Problem" class engines were all fitted with the scoops necessary to take water at high speed and consequently were the first locomotives capable of sustained high speed running. One of the class with the more romantic name Lady of the Lake was awarded a bronze medal at the Exhibition of 1862. In all, sixty of these locomotives were built and as a class they proved themselves to be fast, reliable and remarkably long lived in service. When in late 1861 McConnell resigned from the Southern Division, the premises at Wolverton became the London and North Western Railway's carriage works and Ramsbottom was appointed locomotive superintendent at Crewe, responsible for all of the LNWR's motive power. Ramsbottom largely left McConnell's 'Bloomers' alone

RIGHT
Cornwall in its original 1851 guise.

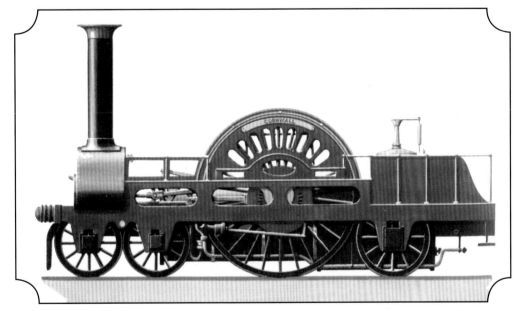

Further Developments

as they were still capable of keeping time with the London to Birmingham expresses. However, most of the Allan or Trevithick locomotives of the Northern Division, with the exception of Cornwall which was rebuilt, were soon scrapped in favour of his own "Problem" class engines. For freight work Ramsbottom built a 0-6-0 tender known as the "DX Goods" of which no less than 943 were built between 1855 and 1872. These engines were simple yet strong and robust and, with a few modifications, the class had a long service life with some examples still working up until 1930.

The Great Northern Railway was incorporated in 1846 to build a line from London to York via Grantham, Retford and Doncaster, and by 1852 this was completed all the way to their London terminus at King's Cross. Engines to work the line were built by R & W Hawthorn and Co. of Newcastle, an experienced firm who had built engines for Timothy Hackworth of the Stockton and Darlington. For the Great Northern they built twenty 2-2-2 locomotives which were updated versions

ABOVE
Henri Giffard's steam propelled airship, for which he invented the injector.

RIGHT
The first of the Stirling Singles, No. 1, which is now kept at York.

of the "Patentee". Later they built a further batch of similar but much larger 2-2-2 engines that became known, inevitably, as "Large Hawthorns". Built with six foot six inch driving wheels and large boilers, these engines were excellent express passenger locomotives of their day, and were entrusted with the London to York section of the new Flying Scotsman passenger service out of King's Cross. At Retford the line was crossed by the Manchester, Sheffield and Lincolnshire Railway and on one occasion a signalling error allowed a MSLR freight train to lumber its way over the crossing, directly in the path of a "Large Hawthorn" at the head of an express bound for York. The Great Northern driver, realising that he had no hope of stopping his train, threw open the regulator and ploughed into the freight train at full speed. The lightly built timber wagons shattered to matchwood but the "Large Hawthorn" kept her feet and the express carried on safely northward.

The Flying Scotsman service was created to provide an express link from London to Edinburgh via the Great Northern Railway from London to York, the North Eastern Railway from York to Berwick and the North British Railway from Berwick to Edinburgh. An obvious requirement was to make the journey time as short as possible and to this end the GNR locomotive superintendent, Archibald Sturrock, designed a still larger locomotive in the hope of reducing the travelling time to eight hours. Built by R & W Hawthorn in 1853, this engine had two pairs of leading wheels and single driving wheels seven feet in diameter. Unfortunately it was too large and too heavy and due to the rigid wheelbase of the leading axles showed some tendency for derailment. The wheels were later removed and replaced in a bogie which considerably improved the engine and she worked until 1870 though no more were built.

One of the most celebrated locomotive designs ever must surely be the eight foot diameter single drivers built by new Great Northern Locomotive Superintendent Patrick Sterling in 1870. Rightly described as a 'work of art' they were a most handsome, efficient, reliable and very fast express

Further Developments

passenger locomotive. Of the 4-2-2 wheel arrangement, they had a leading four wheel bogie with a long wheelbase, outside cylinders and a large firebox supported by the trailing wheels. The large domeless boiler with the elegant brass safety valve cover was one of the most visually striking features of these engines which saw great service on the London to York section of the Flying Scotsman express. On a number of occasions the 'Stirling Singles' were timed at speeds of up to seventy-five miles per hour. Fifty-three of the class were built and they were the mainstay of the GNR's express traffic until the closing years of the nineteenth century when the increasing weight of the

trains demanded still larger engines. The 'Stirling Singles' were all withdrawn by 1916 though the first, No. 1, has been preserved at the National Railway Museum at York.

The Midland Railway was formed in 1844 from a number of smaller railways including the Midland Counties Railway, the North Midland Railway and the Birmingham

and Derby Junction Railway. From 1853 many railways were experimenting with various means by which they could burn coal instead of coke including complicated firebox designs, boilers with combustion chambers and weird and wonderful grates. The Midland Railway instead came up with the idea of having a brick arch placed in the firebox, a baffle plate at the top of the firehole and a fire door which could be used to control the flow of cold air into the firebox. These devices used in conjunction with a steam operated 'blower' that directed a stream of air through the firebox and up the chimney proved to be all that was required to ensure that a coal fired locomotive would 'consume its own smoke'. The locomotive superintendent, Matthew Kirtley, was also one of the first to design an express passenger locomotive with more than one pair of driving wheels. In 1870, as a development of the previous similar though smaller engines, he designed the '800 class'. These were 2-4-0s with outside frames, inside cylinders and two pairs of coupled driving wheels six feet eight inches in diameter. Free steaming and steady riding the '800 class' locomotives were a firm favourite with their crews, and they proved to be fast and reliable operators of the Midland's Anglo-Scottish express traffic. A year later Kirtley introduced a similar engine with a larger boiler and with the driving axle bearings inside the frames. These were the '890 class', some of which were especially modified with a centre buffer at the rear of the tender to enable them to haul the new American Pullman cars first imported by the Midland Railway. The forty-eight members of the '800 class' had long working lives, the ast being scrapped in 1936 after more than sixty years' service.

Chapter Eight

Competition in the South

As we have already seen there was considerable competition between the various railway companies for the prestige, and the ticket revenue, of having the best and fastest express between London and the Scottish cities. Such rivalry also existed between the southern railway companies who competed for traffic from London to the various ports on the south coast. Heavier, more comfortable trains with dining cars and sleeping cars required larger and more powerful locomotives. The single driver was still the most usual arrangement for express passenger engines, with larger boilers, higher working pressures and increased cylinder size giving each successive design progressively more power and speed.

The London and South Western Railway was first incorporated in 1839 and opened lines to Southampton and Portsmouth in 1840 and 1842 respectively. It was not long before the LSWR began to look further afield, to Salisbury, Bournemouth, Exeter, Plymouth and even the Cornish coast. This was, of course, Great Western territory, and the LSWR had to build some sprightly engines to compete with the famed broad gauge locomotives of Daniel Gooch. During his time as LSWR locomotive superintendent Joseph Beattie built a number of 2-4-0

express locomotives for the London to Salisbury and the London to Bournemouth services. Introduced between 1859 and 1860 these engines gave good service despite suffering somewhat from their creator's passion for gadgets. The fireboxes were complicated affairs with 'mid-feathers', an early form of thermic syphon, and different combustion chambers designed to get the maximum amount of steam out of every last ounce of coal. For even greater thermal efficiency, Beattie had devised a way of heating the boiler feed water with exhaust steam from the cylinders. Unfortunately the boilers proved to be prone to leakage and the saving in coal was outweighed by the cost of the extra maintenance required to keep the engines running. Joseph Beattie was succeeded by his son, William Beattie, who, following some unsuccessful experiments with piston valves (he was a little ahead of his time), was replaced by William Adams in 1878. Adams was an experienced locomotive engineer having previously been locomotive superintendent for the North London and the Great Eastern Railways before joining the LSWR, and he soon began to produce express engines able to maintain the scheduled services from London.

There was another railway company

BELOW
Waterloo main line
platform. In the
background is a
Beattie locomotive
on the London and
South Western
Railway, 1870.

competing for the lucrative traffic to Portsmouth and that was the London, Brighton and South Coast Railway. Incorporated in 1846 as a result of the combination of the London and Brighton and the London and Croydon Railways, the LBSC spread its tentacles as far as Portsmouth in the west and Hastings in the east. While their lines to Brighton and the important port at Newhaven enjoyed a complete monopoly the railway was often engaged in sometimes fierce rivalry with both the London and South Western and the London, Chatham and Dover Railway to the east. The LBSC ensured their public image was kept up to scratch by successive generations of superb locomotives renowned not only for their innovation of design and fine performances

but also for their generally striking appearance. After Joy's "Jenny Lind"'s, the most celebrated creations of the succeeding locomotive superintendent, John Craven, were his 2-2-2 engines with six foot six inch single driving wheels built in 1862. Later engines of the LBSC were particularly noted for their outstanding livery of "improved engine green", actually a shade of yellow ochre, introduced by William Stroudley, locomotive superintendent from 1870 to 1889. The colourful paintwork was far from Stroudley's only contribution, he was also one of the first locomotive engineers to give some thought to the standardisation of parts and fittings that could be made common to the various classes of engines in his charge. His first designs included the "Terrier"'s, small but useful and long lived 0-6-0 tank engines, and a 2-2-2 express engine with six foot

nine inch driving wheels named Grosvenor. On one of its trials this engine hauled a train of twenty-two coaches from Brighton to London without any loss of time. A further development of the 2-2-2 type led to the twenty-four strong "G" class with six foot six inch driving wheels introduced in 1881 for the London to Portsmouth expresses. These engines turned in quite remarkable performances over the sometimes steeply graded line across the North Downs, a duty they continued to fulfil until the early years of the twentieth century. With train loads gradually getting heavier Stroudley had to build a more powerful locomotive for the important London to Brighton expresses. His success with the "G" class led him to try a 0-4-2 wheel arrangement with two pairs of driving wheels the same size as those of the "G", namely six foot six inches.

LEFT
A preserved 0-4-2 Gladstone at York decorated for Queen Elizabeth II's Silver Jubilee in 1977.

RIGHT
Dugald Drummond's T9 4-4-0s were introduced in 1899 on the L&SWR.

The first of these engines, Gladstone, was completed in 1882 and attracted some criticism for the unusual wheel arrangement. However, in service Gladstone proved to be fast and extremely powerful for her size and, in spite of the concerns over the leading coupled driving wheels, she was smooth running and rode well at speed. A further thirty-five "Gladstone"s were built, one of which, Edward Blount, was shown at the Paris Exhibition in 1889 and won a gold medal. The "Gladstone"s in their striking ochre livery became the best known of all Stroudley's locomotives. They had a long working life, the last one was not withdrawn until 1932, and the first of the class is preserved at the National Railway Museum at York.

It seems that some of the success of the "Gladstone"s' design rubbed off onto the rival LSWR camp at Nine Elms. William Adams produced a similar 0-4-2 design from the company workshops in 1887, Queen Victoria's Jubilee year, the class being subsequently known as the "Jubilees". Intended for mixed traffic duties they had slightly smaller driving wheels than the "Gladstone"s, six foot rather than six foot six inches, but had the same size cylinders with the steam chests built underneath. With their Adams style stove pipe chimneys and the LSWR's pale green livery they looked quite different, and, like the "Gladstone"s, they were reliable performers and gave many years' service. Indeed the last members of the ninety strong class were still working after World War II and were not scrapped until 1948.

Notwithstanding the success of the "Jubilees", William Adams is probably best remembered for the beautiful 4-4-0 express engines he built for the London and South Western Railway. Sixty of these engines were built between 1891 and 1896, some with six foot seven inch driving wheels and the others with seven foot one inch driving wheels, and they all had outside cylinders with inside slide valves worked by Stephenson's link motion. The engines were built for the London to Bournemouth and London to Exeter expresses, and on these duties they were often timed at speeds of up to eighty miles per hour. The locomotives were fitted with Adams's own design of four wheel leading bogie which he had first patented in 1863, and which gave the 4-4-0s superior riding qualities and great stability at speed. Although these engines began to be withdrawn in 1930 a small number continued in service throughout World War II, and the last one, No. 563, was fortuitously restored for the centennial exhibition at Waterloo station in 1948. This engine is now in the National collection.

Chapter Nine
Railway Rivalry

Competition for traffic between railway companies was often fierce, especially where main line routes were duplicated. The situation was exacerbated where one railway could only reach its destination by means of 'running powers' over a competitor's existing line. Such circumstances could be the cause of anything from the outbreak of fisticuffs that frequently occurred at Havant Station in 1859 when the first LSWR trains tried to reach Portsmouth over LBSC rails, to the building of an entire new line. The Midland Railway, fed up with the delays on the stretch of LNWR metals they had been forced to use to get to Carlisle, built their own line from Settle, creating one of the most celebrated and breathtakingly scenic railways in Britain in the process. The routes north from London to Aberdeen, Glasgow and Edinburgh were particularly fiercely contested. With the LNWR running on the west coast route and the GNR/NER on the east coast, both companies used their considerable publicity machines to promote their respective superiority. Central to the claims and counter claims was, of course, the creation of the motive power necessary to haul the ever heavier trains at faster and faster speeds to their destination. On the LNWR Ramsbottom's "Problem"s of 1859 were still in service and two of them, Waverley and Marmion gave a good account of themselves during the railway 'races' of 1888 when

they ran non stop on the London to Crewe section of the 10.00 a.m. express service to Edinburgh. They were competing with the Great Northern's 10.00 a.m. Flying Scotsman service from King's Cross to York hauled by the fast and powerful eight foot singles of Patrick Stirling. Further north the challenge was taken up on the east coast by the North Eastern Railway from York to Berwick and by the North British Railway from Berwick to Edinburgh. On the west coast route the LNWR carried on from Crewe to Carlisle, and from there the Caledonian Railway continued on to Edinburgh. The gradual and

BELOW
The Settle to Carlisle line passes through the most breathtaking countryside, still enjoyed by rail travellers today. 'West Country' pacific "City of Wells" hauls an excursion train across the Ribblehead Viaduct.

successive reduction of journey times over each route attracted much public interest, and many of the engineering journals of the day published the train timings achieved by each of the railway companies involved. The west coast route was at a slight disadvantage, however, being both slightly longer and rather steeper in places than the east coast route. Eventually the GNR/NER companies managed to pare the journey down to seven hours twenty-seven minutes inclusive of a twenty-five minute meal break at York, although it is doubtful that the passengers would have thought this minor miracle to be of any great benefit as they bumped along at breakneck speeds in rigid six wheeled coaches. The LNWR just could not compete with this, and in the end common sense prevailed and the rival factions agreed on a minimum journey time of eight and a half hours. For a while.

In 1890 the North British Railway opened their celebrated bridge across the Firth of Forth reducing the distance from Edinburgh to Aberdeen by some thirty miles. Five years later the LNWR reduced the journey time of their overnight train to Aberdeen, and the GNR/NER followed suit with a twenty minute cut in their own overnight schedules. The LNWR responded to this with a further cut of forty minutes and the "Race to Aberdeen" was on. An important element of the LNWR's success was a class of small locomotives designed by John Ramsbottom's successor, Francis Webb, and introduced in 1874. These diminutive 2-4-0s, known as the "Precedent"s, were the first engines to be built with their internal steam passages made as short and as direct as possible. This design feature ensured the "Precedent"s were extremely fast and powerful for their size, and in August 1895 one of the class,

Hardwicke, covered the one hundred and forty-one miles from Crewe to Carlisle at an average speed of sixty-seven miles per hour. True, the train hauled was only seventy tons in weight, but there were some fearsome gradients to overcome including, of course, Shap. On this occasion the entire five hundred and forty mile journey from Euston to Aberdeen was completed in less than nine hours including three stops to change engines, and the average speed achieved overall was sixty-three and a half miles per hour. The event made international news, though the hapless passengers may well have wondered why it was necessary for them to arrive at their destination at five o'clock in the morning! After this momentous run the railway companies decided they had gone far enough and that more sensible timings should be re-introduced before

there was a serious accident. No doubt this decision was a source of great relief to the passengers. One hundred and fifty-five "Precedent"'s were built at Crewe works and they had long and useful lives, the last one being withdrawn in 1932. Hardwicke is preserved as part of the National collection in the railway museum at York.

The Midland Railway had a somewhat different approach to wooing the Anglo-Scottish traffic. From the Pullman Palace Car Company of America sufficient parts were imported to build eighteen Pullman carriages at the Midland's Derby works. In 1874 day and night Pullman services were introduced between St Pancras and Bradford, and when the Settle to Carlisle line was completed in 1876 the Midland was able to offer similar services to Edinburgh. The railway also scrapped their third class

LEFT
The Flying
Scotsman train
leaves King's Cross
station, London.

LEFT
The Flying
Scotsman train
leaves King's Cross
station, London.

BELOW
Hardwicke, a
2-4-0 Precedent,
averaged 67mph
from Crewe to
Carlisle in 1895.

accommodation and re-designated their standard second class coaches as third, thus providing an unprecedented standard of comfort to even the lowest fare-paying passengers. This move did not go down well with the Midland's eastern and western rivals who were eventually forced to follow suit.

The Midland locomotives built to haul the Scottish expresses have already been briefly discussed. They were the two classes of 2-4-0 engines built by Matthew Kirtley known simply as the "800" class and the "890" class. The latter engines were especially adapted with a central buffer to haul the complete Pullman trains on the St Pancras to Bradford services. Later, when the Pullman coaches were split up to work the Scottish services, their buffers were rebuilt with two side buffers as is normal British practice, and the "890" class had their centre buffers removed. Although at this time other railways were almost exclusively using 'single' driver engines for their best expresses, the Midland needed the extra adhesion provided by the

2-4-0s due to the many steep gradients on their lines. The "800" class were particularly well designed and were the prime haulers of the Midland Railway's crack expresses. When Samuel Johnson succeeded Kirtley as the Midland's CME in 1874 he rebuilt these engines with bigger boilers and slightly larger cylinders, though he kept the original frames and motion. He also added a small cab and the Johnson 'signature' of a gracefully tapered brass safety valve cover. In this form one of these engines, No. 815, made a notable run from Carlisle to the summit of Ais Gill, covering the forty-eight and a half miles in fifty-nine minutes. Not so remarkable, one might think when comparing this to the exploits of the 'racing' rivals of the east and west coasts. However, No. 815 was hauling a one hundred and thirty ton train up a total rise of eleven hundred feet, the last eleven miles being a one in one hundred gradient. Such was the Midland Railway. In their rebuilt form the forty-eight members of the "800" class were very popular with engine

Railway Rivalry

crews as they would do anything asked of them. Most of these locomotives had long service lives of some fifty years, many of them passing into LMS service in 1923.

Interestingly, in 1887, after having built four coupled engines for some thirteen years, and at a time when other railways thought such things obsolete, Samuel Johnson designed a 4-2-2 'single' driver express engine with seven foot four inch driving wheels. This change of tack was brought about by the invention of steam sanding gear which gave the locomotive extra adhesion when starting off or climbing a steep gradient, and allowed Johnson to make use of the uncomplicated free running qualities of a 'single driver'. With their graceful lines enhanced by the curves of the running plate

and splashers and finished in the fabulous crimson lake livery adopted by the Midland Railway in the 1880s, these engines were a work of art rivalled only by the Great Northern's Stirling singles. They were also extremely fast and could reach speeds of over ninety miles an hour and maintain average speeds in excess of sixty miles per hour. Like Kirtley's "800"s, the locomotives were popular with their crews as they were smooth riding and light on coal. The engines gained the nickname "Spinners" as sometimes they would slip a little when starting a heavy train, even when the sanding gear was used. The great driving wheels would rotate smoothly without any of the bump and clatter that would be felt and heard while a coupled engine was slipping. A Johnson "Spinner"

MAIN
Staff standing in front of the Southern Railway's Golden Arrow service.

was exhibited at the Paris Exhibition of 1889 and was awarded a gold medal.

As the twentieth century took over from the nineteenth century, so the queen who had presided over that vigorous and inventive era passed on also. While royal patronage had been a prize some railways had gone to extreme lengths to win, it was one of Adams's humble "Jubilees" of 1887 that hauled the funeral train over LSWR metals on 2nd February 1901.

Chapter Ten

Standardisation and Imported Technology

Daniel Gooch of the Great Western Railway imposed a degree of discipline on the seven manufacturers that produced the "Firefly" class between 1840 and 1842. This early example of standardisation continued to be the hallmark of Great Western design from 1903 when Churchward took over from Dean and became CME.

As Dean's chief assistant, Churchward had designed the boiler for the "Atbara" 4-4-0s built in 1900. In order to improve steaming rates without causing foaming in the constricted area above the firebox he used the flat topped Belpaire style boiler. This gave a maximum of water area and steam space over the firebox crown. Steam for the cylinders was drawn from a collector pipe within the Belpaire and not from a dome on the boiler barrel. These locos were deemed unattractive by many.

The next change was the tapering of boiler barrels so that more water was carried at the hot firebox end of the boiler and less at the colder chimney end. This was first done on the "City" class 4-4-0s of 1903. Apart from the very first 4-6-0

No. 100 built before 1903, tapered boilers became the standard type to be fitted on all subsequent main line locomotives.

The tapered boiler with its enlarged space over the firebox was an import from American practice, though the Belpaire shape was a Belgian design named after its inventor. Churchward used a long thirty inch piston stroke and supplied steam by piston valves that were more than half the diameter of the pistons. With a valve gear that gave long travel and direct steam passages there was minimum restriction on the flow of steam into and out of the cylinders at high speeds.

The principle of using steam twice, known as compounding, was being used successfully in France on the Nord Railway, so Churchward bought a four cylindered compound design by de Glehn called La France and did some comparative trials. The Great Western locomotive was No. 171, a 4-6-0 called Albion which had the high boiler pressure of 225 lbs per square inch. La France's boiler pressure was 227 psi. No. 171 showed up well even after it was converted to a 4-4-2 in order to make the comparison fairer. The long stroke pistons seemed to develop as much energy from the steam as was the case on the French locomotive with two stages of compounding. Compounds interpose a second set of cylinders between the first set

and the chimney. The exhaust steam that usually escapes into the sky via the chimney is instead diverted to push again, against larger pistons because of the lower pressure.

The Great Western engine was cheaper,

being a simple, and no great improvement of savings seemed to accrue from the compounding principle. However, the French machine ran very smoothly. Its four cylinders were arranged to drive on two axles. The inside cylinders drove the leading axle, the outside cylinders drove the middle axle. This meant that the opposed big end masses could balance out the tendency of long stroke pistons to transmit up and down and back and forth forces through the axle boxes. In 1905 a further test using No. 40 North Star, a newly built four cylindered "Atlantic" or 4-4-2 with divided drive as above took place. Two more de Glehn compounds of the latest improved design were bought and operated in competition with No. 40. The results showed that expensive compounding did not show sufficient economy over Churchward's four cylinders simple design to warrant a change of policy. As a result the "Star" class fitted with Walschaerts (Belgian) inside

valve gear set the standard Great Western express design for the next fifty years.

Most British locomotives at this time supplied saturated steam to their cylinders. In other words, the steam was not much hotter than the water it rose out of, if the saturated 'wet steam' is reheated on its way to the cylinders. In special elements or thin tubes, the result will be 'dry' or superheated steam at much increased temperatures. This principle was applied after 1905 to all Great Western express locomotives.

Water that is fed into boilers from tenders or tanks was generally to the coolest end of the barrel and into the boiler water. After 1911, all Great Western boilers had the water feed clacks put above the water line, i.e. via top feed fittings, and this was a modern innovation that other railways only adopted many years later. Lastly, Swindon standardised the controls and fittings within locomotive cabs to such a high degree that GWR enginemen were instantly at home in the

LEFT
WP Reid's North British Atlantic of 1906 had a Belpaire firebox and outside axleboxes under the cab.

BELOW
McIntosh's 4-6-0 of 1906 had inside cylinders and Stephenson's valve gear.

cabs of any Swindon built locomotive. The next real push for standardisation resulted from the appointment of Swindon-trained William Stanier as CME to the LMS.

Away from the Great Western Railway the use of parallel boilers continued to create the classic British locomotive that was elegant to the eye and not so "American". Sir John Aspinall's huge 4-4-2s on the Lancashire and Yorkshire Railway, nicknamed "High Flyers", are probably the most typical example of this straight up and down style. The nickname derived from the seven foot three driving wheels was also a good description of this generally top heavy locomotive. Trouble was experienced with hot axle boxes which were inside the frames and too near the ash pan. Around 1915 outside bearings were fitted to the offending trailing wheels.

It would be impossible in a book of this size to mention more than a fraction of the locomotive designs to be found in Britain around this date. There were more than a hundred railway companies! If we continue to compare "Atlantics" however, the North British example built

by W P Reid in 1906 was also a high built locomotive. It had a Belpaire firebox and outside axleboxes under the cab. Although it had outside cylinders the valve gear was, as usual, tucked away between the frames.

The 1903 North Eastern "Atlantics", Class V by William Worsdell, had round topped fireboxes and a large five foot six diameter boiler. From an engine driver's point of view the most nightmarish design must have been another North Eastern "Atlantic" designed by Sir Vincent Raven in 1911. This three cylindered locomotive had all three cylinders in line and drove the front coupled axle. There were three sets of Stephenson's valve driven off six eccentrics with a connecting rod, big end, crank and webs all jammed between the frames and under the five foot six diameter boiler. The poor wretch who had the job of oiling up this part of the engine alone would have attended to at least thirty-two oiling points. All of them within a most congested tangle of machinery.

It is strange that each of these designs features longish but narrow fireboxes. The 4-4-2 wheelbase, like the 4-6-2, allows the designer to place a wide and reasonably deep

firebox over the small trailing wheels. This is, of course, what Ivatt did on the Great Northern. He introduced the first "Atlantic"s to Britain in 1898, but these had narrow fireboxes. His next and very successful design made better use of the opportunity to place a short wide firebox across the frames and trailing wheels. This large boilered class of "Atlantic"s appeared in 1902. The first eighty-one were un-superheated and had balanced slide valves, but the last ten were superheated with piston valves. They were a great success being both fast and strong. No. 251, the first of its class, has been preserved. In 1953 it was coupled to

a preserved small "Atlantic" Henry Oakley hauling a special train to Doncaster, taking 192 minutes to do the 156 mile journey. Ted Hailstone and Bill Hoole were the drivers. On the LBSC Douglas Earle Marsh, one time chief assistant to Ivatt, built two classes of large boilered "Atlantic"s which were almost identical to the Great Northern machines. They were known as classes "H1" and "H2". The "H2"s, built in 1911, were superheated. Marsh's "I3" "Atlantic" tanks had demonstrated the value of superheating when they outperformed LNWR tender engines running between Rugby and Brighton on the 'Sunny South Express'.

RIGHT
A BR Standard class 4, 4-6-0 locomotive.

BELOW
The London North Eastern Railway's Gresley A1 locomotive Sansovino at King's Cross Station.

Finally, here are a couple examples of 'traditional' versus the 'new'. Compare McIntosh's Caledonian Railway "Cardean" class 4-6-0 produced in 1906, with R W Urie's "N15" class 4-6-0 built for the London and South Western Railway in 1918. The "Cardean"s had inside cylinders and Stephenson's valve gear which drove slide valves above the cylinders through rockers. The running plate was low and the coupling rod would disappear within its splashers every half turn of the wheels. David Gibson drove No. 903 for five years and must have been a proud man to have charge of such an impressive machine. The LSWR "N15" class were, in contrast, a very modern concept in 1918. Not only did they expose almost the whole diameter of their driving wheels as a result of the high running plate but all the movements of the Walschaerts valve gear as well. Drivers could oil and examine the valve gear without squeezing between the frames. The "N15"s which had short travel valves and 180 lbs psi boiler pressure were given names and included in the new "King Arthur" class of 4-6-0s designed by R E L Maunsell. His

new engines had 200 lbs psi boiler pressure and long travel valves and were capable of a very occasional ninety mile an hour sprint.

The elegant Edwardian locomotives were robust to a fault. During the 1914-1918 war a large number of 2-8-0 heavy freight locomotives designed by J G Robinson for the Great Central Railway were shipped to Europe together with sixty-nine Great Western Dean goods 0-6-0, and their simple strengths proved invaluable under the terrible operating conditions.

In 1922 Raven and Gresley both produced a three cylindered "Pacific" for their respective railways, the North Eastern and the Great Northern. Raven's "Pacific" was old fashioned with a high parallel boiler, inside Stephenson's valve gears and a firebox area inadequate for the tube length. Gresley's "Pacific" had outside Walschaerts valve gear operating the inside valve through a conjugating system. There was very little to oil up under the boiler. Although Gresley's "A1" was more modern it only fulfilled its potential after it had been altered as a result of lessons learned from comparison with a Great Western "Castle".

Chapter Eleven

Grouping

The Railway Executive Committee had been formed prior to 1914 in order to make the best use of the railway system during World War I. This committee combined the talents of the general managers of the railways during and after the War until 1921. In 1923 over 120 separate railway companies amalgamated into four groups, later known as the 'Big Four', which were to retain their identity until Nationalisation in 1948. The largest of these groups was the London Midland and Scottish Railway, followed by the London and North Eastern Railway, the Great Western Railway and then the Southern Railway which was the smallest of all. The locomotive development policies reflected the tendency of each of the respective CMEs to follow tried and tested formulae where the resulting engines had proved to be economic machines. For the GWR, C B Collett, who had taken over at Swindon after Churchward's retirement in 1921, continued the enlargement of a basic theme with the "Castle" class built in 1924. These engines had four cylinders set out to the 'Swindon taste' and 225 lbs boiler pressure. On 2nd May 1925 No. 4074 Caldicote Castle hauling the 'Cornish Riviera' express ran the 225.7 miles from Paddington to Plymouth in 231.58 minutes with driver Rowe and fireman Cook in the cab. The locomotive did the job at between 19% and

BELOW
A French Wagons-Lits Pullman car from the Paris - Calaise section of the Golden Arrow service to London.

20% cutoffs, and for each pound of coal that Cook threw on the fire ten pounds of water turned to steam. You cannot get much better than that! In fact that sort of efficiency would not be possible without first class Welsh coal which is 90% carbon.

The name of the train gives a clue to the 'luxury theme' of this chapter. Railway travellers were to be tempted away from travel by road by the promise of speed and comfort on the way to exotic places. The inclusion of 'Riviera' in the title of the train put the passenger in mind of a journey to the south of France. Another crack GWR

express was the 'Cheltenham Flyer' which ran at an average speed of seventy miles per hour and was claimed to be "The Fastest Train in the World". A further ruse practised by the wily GWR publicists was to assert that their "Castle"s were the "most powerful class of locomotive in Britain". Tractive effort, which is what this claim was all about, is a figure arrived at by doing sums that take into account the number of cylinders, their size, 85% of the boiler pressure and the driving wheel diameter in inches. At the end of a bit of complicated multiplication and division the tractive effort of the "Castle"s was calculated to be 31,625lbs. This publicity, together with the comparison of the GWR 4-6-0 with an LNER 4-6-2 at the 1924 Wembley

Exhibition sent a widening ripple across the placid pond of British locomotive design.

The LNER CME was the Crewe-trained engineer Nigel Gresley, who had followed the design principles laid out by Ivatt when he built his celebrated large boilered "Atlantic"s. The main drawback of a four coupled design is the lack of adhesion on slippery rails. While keeping the essential proportions of the "Atlantic" Gresley added two more driving wheels and created a fine looking "Pacific", but with a boiler pressure of only 180 lbs, its tractive effort was calculated to be 29,835 lbs. At the Wembley Exhibition the large and racy "Pacific" stood next to a rather small engine around which the 'pressmen' hovered because it was billed as Britain's "most powerful" locomotive.

The LNER countered with the argument that 'power' depended on boiler capacity. Tractive effort only represented the maximum pull possible, and if the engine's boiler was too small the tractive effort would fall off as the boiler pressure dropped. The LNER "Pacific" had the larger boiler and would therefore develop more 'horsepower' at high speeds when a small boiler would tend to become 'winded'. The argument was settled by comparative trials between the two designs in 1925. Driver Young of Old Oak Common was in charge of GWR No. 4079 Pendinnis Castle during the runs on LNER metals that proved the superiority of the Great Western engine.

Subsequently, Gresley increased the boiler pressure of his "Pacific" and lengthened the valve travel, enabling the design to realise its full potential at short cut off.

The LMS were likewise influenced when No. 5000 Launceston Castle again proved her superiority during similar trials on their metals in 1926. To alleviate an obvious problem contact was made with the Southern Railway design team at Ashford, who had incorporated the principle of long travel valves in their latest design of 4-6-0, the "Lord Nelson"'s, which had a tractive effort of 33,590 lbs. Plans of the new design were made available to the LMS which resulted in the creation of Henry Fowler's "Royal Scot" class in 1927. These engines broke

through the Midland 'small engines' policy, though despite a shockingly modern short chimney they retained an old fashioned appearance with their very 'Midland Railway' squareness of style. Later, we shall see how ex-GWR William Stanier, the new CME for the LMS, would improve matters further.

As for the "Lord Nelson" class, experience showed that despite the higher tractive effort the engines were not a great improvement (apart from a smoother ride) over the "King Arthur"s. It was the old argument of tractive effort versus boiler performance, and the "Lord Nelson"s could be finicky for steam. Using Welsh coal, I have fired to "King"s "Castle"s and "Lord Nelson"s and have found that the Great Western engines steamed more reliably. I believe that on the "Lord

Nelson" the brick arch was not at a steep enough angle to the firebars and thus firemen could not keep a sufficient depth of fuel over the centre back of the grate. This problem did not arise with hard, long flame coal.

To counter the new 'most powerful' challenge from the Southern Railway, Swindon produced an enlarged 4-6-0 with a long firebox, longer piston stroke, higher boiler pressure (250 lbs) and smaller driving wheels. The mathematics of this combination gave the new engine a tractive effort of 40,300 lbs. Named after British kings of the realm, this new Great Western class of locomotives was actually born out of a publicity war.

The travelling public were being offered increasingly luxurious, attractively designed

BELOW
Lord Nelson class engines were often tricky to fire, says the author.

RIGHT
The new LMS streamlined locomotive 'Duchess of Gloucester' leaves London's Euston Station on her first long distance journey, 1938.

and exotically named trains, hauled by locomotives that became household names for their power and speed. Pullman car trains ran on the Southern from Victoria to the continental ports. The Golden Arrow headboard and insignia graced locomotive 'front ends' on both sides of the Channel. The Bournemouth Belle ran out of Waterloo, the Queen of Scots from King's Cross to Edinburgh. Eventually streamlined coaches hauled by streamlined locomotives, with record speeds being attained and surpassed, were run by both the LNER and the LMS as the two companies vied for the Anglo-Scottish traffic as their predecessors had, barely forty years before. The 'Race to the North' was on again.

The round-topped boilers of Doncaster were competing against the Belpaire boilers of Crewe. William Stanier, recruited from his position as assistant to Collett on the GWR in 1931, was finally able to change the 'small engine' policy of the Midland-dominated LMS. His predecessors, Hughes and Fowler, had not been so lucky. In 1933 Stanier's first "Princess" class "Pacific" No. 6200 Princess Royal was built at Crewe. Bearing some resemblance to a GWR "King", she had a wider firebox with a pony truck underneath. The layout of the four cylinders was identical to the "King"s but with four sets of Walschaerts valve gears operating the piston valves. In 1936 No. 6201 Princess Elizabeth hauled seven coaches non stop the 401 miles from Euston to Glasgow at an average speed of seventy miles per hour. Driver Laurie Earl on 'improved' "Pacific" No. 6206 hauled sixteen coaches weighing 500 tons from Euston to Rugby, covering the 82.6 miles in 83.4 minutes.

In 1937 larger boilered "Pacific"s with six foot nine inch driving wheels were produced to Stanier's design. Initially named "Coronation"s and later known as the "Duchess" class, they were originally

Grouping

LEFT
One of the A4
Pacifics was named
'Sir Nigel Gresley'
after its designer.

RIGHT
The A4 class
pacific locomotive
'Dominion of New
Zealand' leaving
King's Cross
Station, London.

built with streamlined casings painted blue with white striping that matched the design of the 'Coronation Scot' train. Built with larger fireboxes than the "Princesses", they had the same boiler pressure and larger driving wheels giving them a tractive effort of 40,000 lbs. Only two sets of Walschaerts valve gears were fitted, these were outside the frames and operated the inside valves through rocker arms in a reversal of the method used on the Great Western "Kings". To help the fireman a steam operated coal pusher was fitted in the tender.

The "Duchess" class had been built at a time of intense competition between the LMSR's west and the LNER's east coast routes to the north. In 1934 Gresley's improved "Pacific" No. 4472 Flying Scotsman was timed at 100 mph. Then the streamlined "A4" No. 2509 Silver Link hauling the 'Silver Jubilee' streamlined express topped 112.5 mph down Stoke bank. On 29th June 1937 LMS "Pacific" No. 6220 Coronation hauling the eight coaches of the 'Coronation Scot' express reached 114 mph just two miles outside Crewe. They had to stop at Crewe! There were 20 mph speed restrictions on the approach as set by the signalmen. With the brakes full

on they were still doing 105 mph with one mile to go. At 56 mph they went over the 20 mph pointwork without coming off the rails and succeeded in coming safely to rest in the platform at Crewe station. It was obvious that this had been an exuberant and hazardous attempt at the speed record which, while successful, could have had terrible consequences. Express locomotives do not have to have strong brakes as the train stops the locomotive. There were only twelve brake blocks on the 164 ton "Pacific" and there were sixteen brake blocks to each thirty ton coach. Drivers were instructed not to exceed sixty miles per hour when running 'light engine' i.e. with no coaches. The 'Coronation Scot' and its locomotive had a total weight of 434 tons, 164 tons of which were inadequately braked at speeds above sixty miles per hour. I doubt that the outcome would have been the same under modern track maintenance regimes.

With the long descent from Stoke offering their trains plenty of space the LNER set a record that the LMS could not top. In July 1938 Joseph Duddington drove the streamlined "A4" Mallard up to a speed of 126 miles per hour on a special 'brake test' run. This record has never been beaten by a steam locomotive.

An interesting practical comment here. It is not difficult to make a locomotive go extremely fast. It is quite difficult to make them go faster than 100 miles per hour plus the figure you are aiming to exceed. Speed settles on a plateau, there is no precise formula or setting of controls that will ensure a given speed. Locomotives have a natural galloping action, though some run more freely than others. The space ahead is swallowed up amazingly quickly while the driver tries a shorter cutoff, finds no increase in speed, then tries a longer cutoff. Has the speedo reacted? If it has not another mile has flashed beneath the wheels during his thirty-five seconds of indecision. There were no further challenges to be met from the LMSR.

The Southern did not go in for record-breaking high speed exploits. However, the air-smoothed "Pacific"'s designed by O V S Bulleid in 1941, which were fitted with his chain driven miniature Walschaerts valve gear operating in an oil bath, were capable of topping 100 miles per hour and did so right up to the final days of steam on the Southern in 1967.

A world war soon ended those exciting summertime races. Competitive displays of finery became no more than memories that warmed the spirits through the grey years ahead.

Chapter Twelve

World War II

William Stanier's assistant from 1933, Robert Riddles, had immense practical experience of the problems that fitters and engine crews faced in their daily tasks. He had been present on the footplates of the LMS "Pacific"s when they were road tested in 1935 and also during the record long distance trials of 16th November 1936, and the high speed runs of June 1937. He had acted as fireman and driver during the 'Coronation Scot's tour of America in 1939. He had coped with hot axle boxes, melted cross head slippers, collapsed brick arches and poor coal. It is doubtful that any other man had brought so much useful experience to the job of designing steam locomotives. At the outbreak of war in 1939, Robert Riddles was given the job of heading the Directorate of Transportation Equipment. The Great Western Dean goods 0-6-0s of 1883 had once again been sent to Europe earlier that year. In 1941 he sent 91 Robinson 2-8-0s to the Middle East, all of which were to remain there. The urgent need for heavy goods engines for Britain's war effort was met by a large order for Stanier 2-8-0s. Brighton works produced one of these a week, they built

93 in all. Two hundred and eight of these engines were built for the War Department, most of which went to the Middle East after Europe had been overrun by the Germans.

Because Stanier's locomotives were fairly sophisticated they required scarce materials and time to build them. Riddles designed an 'Austerity' engine that was cheaper to make. The North British Locomotive Company in Glasgow had built the Fowler 'Royal Scot's, and with their co-operation Riddles worked out a simple design. For cheapness and ease of construction, Riddles gave them round topped, parallel boilers, and he substituted cheaper metals for some of the castings. They had outside Walschaerts valve gear, two cylinders, boiler pressure of 225 lbs and a narrow grate. The cab and footplates were very plain with no frills. The first of these engines came out in January 1943. It had taken ten days to put together and five months had elapsed from the placement of the order. The North British built them at the rate of five per week, 935 in total being

built, with 450 lent to the four railway companies until the engines were needed overseas. The design was a great success.

An engine was later requested with an axle loading of only 13.5 tons. Riddles decided on a 2-10-0. He made the tread of the centre driving wheel wide but flangeless. This enabled the locomotive to run through four and a half chain curves without excessive friction. These engines were given wide fireboxes of forty square feet. However, the war had ended before the first of the 150 such engines ordered were built by the North British Locomotive Company. A large number of shunting engines based on a Hunslett-designed saddle tank were also produced for the War Department. These engines were strong but simple, and strong but simple continued to be the theme of the subsequent locomotives designed by Riddles that we will get to meet in the next chapter.

On his return to the LMS at the end of the war, R A Riddles was appointed Vice President (Engineering) of the company.

Chapter Thirteen

Nationalisation and BR Standard Locomotives

In January 1948 the four railway companies were taken over by the government, and British Railways was created. Compensation was paid to the shareholders. The former CMEs, Peppercorn, Bulleid, Hawksworth and Ivatt, were replaced by R A Riddles, who was made the mechanical and electrical engineer responsible to the newly created Railway Executive. Riddles had started out as an apprentice on the LNWR at Crewe in 1909, and had worked his way up as we saw in the previous chapter, to Vice President (Engineering) of the LMS. His flair for organisation and design were now to be tested as he worked to combine the skills and temperaments of the four railway locomotive design teams.

Locomotive design on the Great Western had been stagnant for many years. On the Southern, Bulleid was seen to be going off on a tangent with his "Leader" project, and Peppercorn on the North Eastern was developing his large modernised "Pacific"s which, however, retained the traditional Doncaster round-topped firebox. The LMS under Ivatt had thoroughly embraced labour saving innovations, for example,

self-cleaning smoke boxes and fully rocking grates with hopper ash pans. The Ivatt 2-6-0s and 2-6-2 tanks were very up to date though small machines that replaced the ancient 0-6-0s formerly in service.

CMEs usually relied on their chief draughtsmen to do the detail work on proposed new locomotive projects. The name of the CME that produced the design often hid the name of the man or men that gave actual shape to the locomotive in question, thereby making it recognisable as the CME's style. So it was with Riddles, who brought together the chief draughtsmen of Derby, Swindon, Brighton and Doncaster in order to discuss and give advice for the new range of Standard locomotives suitable for all line usage. Of course, the ex-LNWR Crewe apprentice could not resist having almost all of Britain's locomotive fleet painted black. The locomotive trials of September 1948 were used to test the strengths and weaknesses of the engines then available, the results of which revealed no great differences.

The largest of the proposed classes was a Class 8 "Pacific" and the smallest some Class 3 2-6-2 tanks. The year 1948 was one during

RIGHT
A Nationalisation poster going up at Waterloo, giving notice of the passing of control of the railways to the British Transport Commission.

which the British economy was under great strain, the winter was a hard one and the effects of the last war were still very evident. Ration books were still being used in 1951. I remember that as a shift worker I was entitled to an extra two ounces of cheese on my ration book for sandwiches for work. Riddles published the comparative costs of building steam locomotives as opposed to diesel or electric locomotives. Electric locos were double the cost, plus the cost of the lineside power supply, and diesels were four times the cost of steam. The coal fields of Britain were very accessible but oil had to be imported, and hydro-electric power supplies were not an option. So it was that in January 1951 a brand new very American looking 'Pacific' locomotive made its appearance, and was named "Britannia". Riddles and his team were clever; the new machine was different enough not to be an example of any of the previous main line express engines. To suit the austerity of the time the engine was designated a 'mixed traffic' locomotive. She was a Class 7 and had features that were culled from the best practices of the four constituent railways. One could see elements of the North Eastern in the slide bars and valve gear and the boiler and frames were Bulleid. The smokebox and many of the cab fittings, including window catches, were from the very practical designs of Swindon. The reverser, though working fore and aft like a grocer's bacon slicer, had the gearing of an LMS loco and the regulator handle, like that of a Bulleid or GN "Pacific" was the pull-out kind. The clean, uncluttered backhead was more like a Western or a North Eastern loco than an LMS design. On an LMS loco it is difficult to clean the backhead as closely packed hot and intrusive control valves

scorch the wrists of unwary enginemen.

Riddles had achieved this by giving aspects of the design to the draughtsmen of Brighton, Derby, Swindon and Doncaster. The "Britannia" was built at Crewe and with fourteen others of the class were sent to work on the Great Eastern line out of Liverpool Street, and a further ten went to the GWR.

BELOW
A Class 3 2-6-2 on shunting duty at Waterloo.

The truly innovative features included no fall plate between the engine and tender, which gave a firm base on which to stand when firing. The cab was supported on cantilevers off the back of the boiler so that the fit of the cab was tighter and less draughty than on previous designs which had to allow for the expansion and contraction of the boiler in and out of the cabs. Regulator rodding was external to the boiler so that glands were not made too tight by the attempts to prevent drips and blows into the cab. There were small windows in the tender front for dust-free backwards running and quite good seats too. But they were essentially very simple locomotives: only two

cylinders, no steam operated reversers, no electric lighting, and so back to the old oil lamps for Southern and North Eastern crews who had become used to better illumination.

One modern feature that had been tried on the LMS by Ivatt was the fitting of roller bearings to the axles. This made the engine very free running indeed! The handbrake, which was an LMS bevelled gear design and never very efficient, had to be forced on very hard or the engine toddled off when its crew had parked it in the shed.

The roller bearings, curiously enough, make these engines hard and noisy to ride on. There is no give on the hard steel rollers. The 9F produced later has old fashioned white metalled axle boxes and the ride is

quieter and softer than that of a "Britannia".

Predictably, Great Western crews compared the new locomotives unfavourably with their own designs. They found them noisy and draughty, they complained that the coal was blown off the shovel because there was no fall plate; this was despite the fact that Great Western tender locos have no cab doors! All Western locos are fired from the left side of the cab, the firemen fire right handed. The Standard locos, like every other engine built since 1940, were fired left handed from the right side of the cab, and drivers sat where most station platforms and signals are, on the left. The Western men said that their backs hurt when they shovelled from a shovel plate instead of from two inches lower than

BELOW
A rebuilt Southern 'West Country' class 4-6-2.

RIGHT
The class 7 Britannia was a modern and clever design.

their boots as they had done before. They did not get on with the technique needed in order to get coal into the back corners of the wide firebox. On Western locos the fireboxes are quite narrow, though long, and the Western shovel had a very long blade which was filled to excess before whacking the coal through the firehole door. They did not have to aim, just whack. Now they had to twist that great blade to one side or the other, and it was not easy for them. They also complained that the smoke deflectors obscured the driver's view forward. It should be noted that Great Western engines, having sharply tapered boilers with the taper on the top, give the driver an extremely good forward view and have never needed smoke deflectors to lift the steam. The new engine's boiler was tapered at the bottom

which did not give as good a view forward.

Elsewhere, crews were happy with the new design, which was seen as a fairly primitive substitute for existing multi-cylindered express locos, and a vast improvement on some of the 4-6-0s of the Great Eastern section of the Eastern region. Speeds of over ninety miles per hour were to be recorded behind "Britannia" "Pacific"s. Preparation and disposal duties were made easy by the lack of inside valve gears, the roller bearings and rocking and drop grates. Strangely, the self-cleaning smokebox did not work with the Welsh coal burned at Nine Elms. The excessively dusty coal which filled our tenders went straight through the tubes only partly burned, and piled up against the mesh so that it was almost up to the top of the door and had to be shovelled out by hand or the engine would not steam next trip.

This also happened on the class 5 4-6-0s that were built at Doncaster to replace the old "King Arthur"'s, and which even took the names of some of the Urie "Arthur"'s. The class 5s were fast and strong. Like all BR Standard locos they lost their zip if the boiler pressure went below 200 lbs. They were essentially a Stanier "Black 5" with modern features. The roller bearings made them harsh and rattly to work on. They did not steam as well on Welsh dust as our "King Arthur"'s did, so we had some worrying moments. I discovered, after firing on a "Castle" to Plymouth, that if you filled the box ridiculously high with a great 'haycock', like a "Castle", and kept whacking the stuff in over the half door, steaming could be improved.

The smaller class 4 4-6-0s were not as popular as the class 5s because when running at speed the tender would try to overtake the engine. The fore and aft movement caused by the pistons was magnified by slack drawbar buffers. Coal would shuffle out of the coal hatch and rattle noisily onto the steel footplate. Eventually someone earned themselves a £25.00 prize for suggesting that a coal door flap be fitted, they did not run freely or steam very well and double chimneys were fitted to many of the Southern based engines. The mostly steel footplate was a feature of Standard locos that contributed to the noise and coldness of the cabs.

The 2-6-4 class 4 tanks that were built at Brighton were based on a Stanier design and were extremely good. They were used to replace elderly 4-4-2 tanks on short distance passenger work. They rode as smoothly as

a coach. They did not have roller bearings. They were as easy to drive in reverse as they were chimney first, and it is difficult to see why Bulleid was so convinced that the double ended "Leader" would be any improvement on a modern 2-6-4 tank which could handle intensive passenger services, in and out of termini, with ease.

The smallest of the BR Standard designs were not disguised by having Continental/American style running plates, but were as Ivatt had made them for the LMS. These were fine, practical locomotives and they became everyone's favourite. The detail work for the very popular heavy goods loco, the class 9F 2-10-0, was done by Jarvis at Brighton. These engines ran smoothly and faster than might be expected bearing in mind their massive cylinders and five foot driving wheels. The boiler was pitched as high as the loading gauge would permit in order that a wide firebox could be put over the trailing driving wheel and still be deep enough to hold the depth of fire required to withstand the pull of the exhaust. As a result, some of the boiler fittings, dome, mudhole door clamps etc are pared down so as to clear tunnels and bridges. With such a small dome it became apparent that water could enter the regulator valve if the boiler was filled to the normal level. The water gauges were given false 'top nuts' that partially obscured the top third of the glass, so that firemen had only filled the glass two-thirds though it appeared to be full. When water enters the regulator it can result in an uncontrollable slip: this once happened under a footbridge on which children were standing. The blast from the chimney blew out the planking and the children fell to their deaths.

The 9Fs were made very flexible,

RIGHT
The Standard class 4 4-6-0 was not popular with some drivers because it was cold and noisy.

despite the five driving axles, by the same method that Riddles had used on his WD 2-10-0s of World War II. The centre driving wheels had no flange and could roll 'steam roller like' across the head of the rail on tight curves. Like the "Crab" 4-6-0s of the LMS, the cylinders being of a large diameter were inclined steeply at the leading end so as to give sufficient clearance when entering curving platforms.

Because of the driving wheels below the firebox the ash pan is also shallow at its outer edges and so limiting the flow of air to the edges of the fire. The firebed is only six inches in depth when the coal is level with the bottom of the fire door ring. With a heavy load and with Welsh coal the fire needed to be up to the level of the top of the door opening to make these engines steam. This I found out when my fireman was puzzled that the engine was not steaming with the fire at a height usually carried on our Bulleid "Pacific"s. He then doubled the depth and it worked, and we had no more trouble.

The missing Class 8 Standard 4-6-2 was built in 1954 as a result of the terrible collision that took place at Harrow in December 1952. This had involved three trains and destroyed three locomotives, one of which was the newly rebuilt Turbomotive renamed Princess Anne. I took my first look at this impressive machine at the International Railway Congress exhibition. It was about the same size as a "Merchant Navy" and had three cylinders that were supplied steam by the Caprotti valve gear. This undramatic gear looks like propshafts on a large car, for instance there is no little 'dance' of the combination lever, no rocking of the

LEFT
Class 9F 2-10-0 Evening Star was the last steam locomotive to be built in the UK, in 1960.

expansion links as a result of the ducking and diving of return cranks and eccentric rods. Its poppet valves separate the events that give 'cut off' from the event that opens up the exhaust route to the chimney.

In comparison with the "Britannia"'s which have a firebox of a similar size to a "West Country", Duke of Gloucester (the new engine's name) had a firebox with the grate area of a "Merchant Navy", i.e. 48.5 square feet. Everything else was

typical of the Standard locomotives that were already in service. However, the new engine was never popular with its crews. It was unlikely to be the equivalent of the mighty four cylindered "Duchesses", though it should have been as good as a good three cylindered rebuilt "Royal Scot". It is highly probable that as it was the only engine of its type, no-one ever got used to driving it. But more of this engine later.

Chapter Fourteen

Steam in Decline 1954 to 1968

The Conservative Government of 1954 decided that steam power had to go. It may have been seen as a symbol of the 'socialist' nationalisation of railways that had taken place in 1948. Under this nationalisation the management had publicly declared their support for steam.

I was doing my National Service at this time and will never forget the dismay that I felt on reading in the Sunday newspapers the coming end of steam traction on Britain's railways. At nineteen years of age I had been a fireman at Nine Elms when I was called up, now it seemed that I would have no job to return to at the end of my army service. I was 'Gloomy Groomey' that day! The decline of steam will therefore be a somewhat personal account.

Luckily for me the changeover to diesel and electric traction was not to be finally accomplished until 1968. In the meantime I was able to experience the declining years of steam on the footplates of most of the great express locomotive classes that were hauling trains north, south, east and west during that period. At the age of thirty I was delighted to find myself a driver in number three link at Nine Elms, which involved runs to Bournemouth and Salisbury, and boat trains to Southampton docks. During this period I was therefore driving examples of Bulleid's original "Pacific"'s and comparing them to the rebuilt engines as modified by the Brighton drawing office under Jarvis.

The decline of steam was to be more prolonged than was forecast in 1954. The five express diesel locomotives, two of them LMS designs by Ivatt, the other three Southern designs by Bulleid, had been allocated to the Southern Region for a short time before being transferred to the Midland Region. As a result, contrary to simple logic the most 'modern', i.e. the most electrified railway, retained express steam services on its South Western section, long after the 'less modern' railways had gone over to diesel or electric traction.

Before I left the army I was privileged to meet Bill Hoole of King's Cross, and he, knowing how I missed the footplate life, (as the Army had decided that a fireman would be better used as a lorry driver) provided me with his roster months ahead. This was so that I could ride with him on the North Eastern "Pacific"'s to Grantham and Newcastle. The "Deltic"'s were now taking over some of the duties and I was delighted at the opportunity to learn more of my craft

RIGHT
Britain's first main line diesel train leaving St Pancras for a test run to Derby and Manchester. The locomotive's designer H A Ivatt is climbing on board, 1948.

on the fine "Pacific"s that would soon be displaced forever. Bill's regular engine at the time was No. 60007 Sir Nigel Gresley, but it was on No. 60008 Dwight D Eisenhower that I had my first memorable trip.

It was on 19th April 1955 when I fired the 10.40 a.m. King's Cross to Peterborough while Bill's mate took a break back in the train. The corridor tender

enabled this swap to take place. Later, at Grantham, we had some food before taking over the engine which had been turned and serviced. The train that we now headed was the up Flying Scotsman which had arrived fifteen minutes late.

The "A4"s are a 'powerpack' enclosed in a small and graceful shape. Within the cab the low footplate with its raised

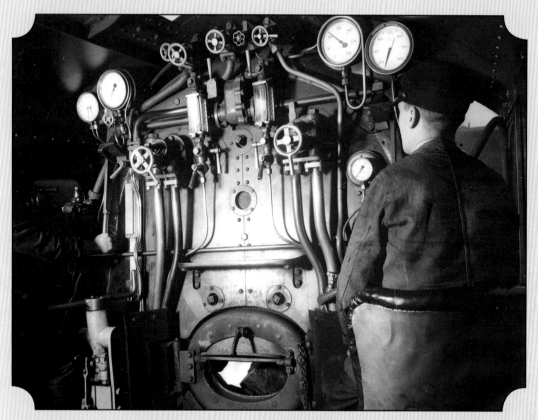

floorboards to the left and right of the firing level, accentuates the height of the backhead. The water gauges are above the average man's head and you climb up to the driver's bucket seat. This is in contrast to Southern "Pacific"s where you stand higher up the boiler and the cab roof is nearer to your head. Externally though, an "A4" seems no larger than a "West Country".

Bill's fireman made up his fire a little and we were off. The power displayed over the next hundred miles was blood tingling! Bill worked her on full regulator and at 'cut offs' ranging from between 35% up hill and 12% on the level. We reached a top speed of ninety-one miles per hour at Essendine (timed from the train) with the boiler pressure down a little at 200 lbs.

In contrast to the Southern methods on Bulleid's engines, the water was seldom more than halfway up the glass and the firebed was so thin that its surface 'danced' under the exhaust blast. We arrived in King's Cross (after suffering two signal checks and observing the speed restriction through Peterborough) two minutes early! I was stone deaf when I got off the engine after 101 minutes of incredible noise. Within the cab Bill and his mate relaxed again, a job well done. The hot engine smelled of scorched metal as the firedoor cooled off, and every pin on the valve gear exuded the aroma of warm rape oil. Like a thoroughbred horse 60008 stood with her nose to the buffers while I took a last admiring gaze.

As a result of trips like this I modified my

LEFT
The footplate of
a steam locomotive.

BELOW
These are two
examples of
express engines
the author used
to drive. In front
is 35004 Cunard
White Star, an
unrebuilt Bulleid
Pacific. Behind is
a rebuilt version of
the same class.

firing technique on the rebuilt "Merchant Navy" engines. They were fitted with baffle plates as the steam operated firedoor mechanism had been taken off. The baffle plate made it very difficult to keep a really deep fire at the back of the box. Most firemen would not put the baffle in. I reasoned that where a baffle was supplied, non usage could be used to deny compensation for scalding if a tube burst. I tried the shallow fire I had seen used on the "A4"s and "A3"s and it worked. And I could do it with the baffle in place. However, this resulted in many long faces on the firemen that took over from me at Salisbury. It was years later that I realised that the evil smelling oil that often drenched the hot firedoors of the engines I took over on the up trains to London were an attempt to 'punish' me for not handing over box-fulls of fire to them on the down trains!

The "West Country"s really did like great haycock fires just inside the door, and this was the coolest way to fire them as no heat could escape into the smallish cab. I could make them steam when I had to on six inches of firebed when the coal was 100% dust, by feeding the white hot bed with dust sprayed off the shovel like the mechanical stoker on an American "Big Boy". Bulleid "Pacific" No 34018 loved this treatment as did 35018. Meanwhile on the Western Region nothing had changed since Churchward's day, and engines were always fired with great haycock fires and to excellent effect. This I was to discover when I rode on No. 6012 King Edward VI from Paddington to Plymouth (225.7 miles) on Friday 27th June 1958. We had a load of nine coaches and a van. The train was the 9.30 a.m. semi-fast and its crew came from Old Oak Common shed.

The safety valves were sizzling and shushing within their brass housing as we departed four minutes late, but they became quiet as the pressure dropped back. The haycock fire was not properly alight but fireman, Dai Lloyd, gave it a lift up with a heavy dart and she steamed easily after that with steady and unhurried firing.

Although the "King"s have an eleven

foot six inch firebox the high brick arch and steeply sloping grate allows a fireman to feed the fuel in mainly to the centre and the rear of the box. The heaped fuel, however, works its way forward to keep sufficient firebed depth at the front tubeplate.

There was no shovel plate. The tender floor from which Dai lifted the coal was inches lower than the wooden footplate of the engine. When he had scooped a very full shovel of coal, Dai pulled open the firedoor flap by the chain attached. It would land with a thump on the boards, he then swung the coal into the centre of the box and replaced the flap before sticking the shovel back under the coal in the tender for the next delivery.

This may sound a painfully elaborate way to fire an engine. However, the timing becomes perfect and minimal effort is expended by an experienced man. I fired from Taunton to Newton Abbot, about fifty miles and soon got into the 'swing of it'. The engine rode smoothly and the absence of doors did not make for a draughty cab, though I noticed that GWR

engine men wore their jackets tucked inside their overall trousers, and they wore cycle clips above their boots – to keep out the dust I supposed. The four cylindered loco had quite a bark at the chimney, but with Welsh coal and the heavy fire no destruction of the firebed was apparent.

I was impressed. The cab was always kept spotlessly clean. Both men worked well together and kindly warned me to put a little extra fuel in just before we ran along the sea wall at Dawlish, where the 'views' could be stunning. We arrived at Plymouth right on time and, later that evening I joined Dai and his driver in the Liara Inn. It was full of Welsh enginemen who sang beautifully all evening as we drank away the thirst that only engines can create. At 07.00 a.m. next morning, with a slight hangover, I joined my friends in the cab of "Castle" class No. 7031, Cromwell's Castle for the return trip to London. We had a load of six coaches to Newton Abbot, then twelve on to Paddington. And again the engine did the job nicely. I noted the cabs were painted

RIGHT
At night the shed lighting illuminates a West Country swathed in a wreath of smoke and steam.

BELOW
35027 Portl Line is another engine the author used to drive. It weighed 100 tons – without its tender!

green inside and did not rattle around the boiler. The engines held their water and did not prime when their water was at the top of the glass. We never had to set back in order to start away from stations.

A month later I tried this method of firing on BR Standard 5 4-6-0 73088. My regular mate Len Rickard and I were working a one hundred and seven mile non stop special of ten coaches from Bournemouth to Waterloo. The engine loved that kind of firing. Our passengers gave us a pound each at the end of the trip, my wages then were about ten pounds per week including 'mileage'.

On 30th December 1957 I joined driver Brown and fireman Whittingham in the cab

of 8P 46233, Duchess of Sutherland at the head of the mid-day 'Scot'. We had a load of fourteen coaches equalling 469 tons and a tight eighty minute schedule for the eighty miles to Rugby. The coal mainly consisted of large slabs of hard which spat and crackled from the brimming firebox door. It sounded like a fish and chip fryer as the heat spalled the slate like coal. These large locomotives have quite small cabs and the height of their footplates is a complete contrast to the low footplates of North Eastern engines. My head was often out in the rain and ash when I stood behind the driver, keeping out of the fireman's way as he swung great slabs of coal to right and left back corners of the wide

LEFT
One of steam's dirtiest jobs – throwing ash out of the smokebox of a Pacific express locomotive.

RIGHT
The prototype of the Deltics that eventually replaced Gresley's A4s.

firebox. The boiler pressure, which had been
at 240 lbs, soon fell to 200 and stayed there
all the way to Rugby. The fireman was 'up
against it' as the engine primed with only half
a glass of water. She was not in the best of
health. The engine rode well, though, and
the cab was not dusty. The driver, sitting on
the left, could reach his controls easily and
the brake valve, unlike those on the Great
Western Kings, could be operated while
sitting down and leaning out of the open
window. The long regulator handle closed
itself frequently and it was common practice
to jam a piece of coal in the quadrant to
keep it wide open on the fast stretches.

As was usual on the LMR, the side
windows were dirty enough to be mistaken
for metal. The shovel plate was almost on
the floor, the fall plate between the loco
and tender was humped and divided into

two parts. The ten ton capacity coal space
was cavernous and a steam operated coal
pusher was demonstrated to me and a wall
of coal pressed against the tender front.

At Crewe, my companions went off
with their engine and 46202 Princess Mary
Louise backed onto the train with two
extra coaches, making sixteen in all, equal
to 550 tons. The "Princess" was more
like a large Great Western engine. It had
a smaller square fronted and somewhat
draughty cab. Away we went, two more
Crewe men at the controls, 250 lbs on the
boiler and full regulator with seldom less
than 30% cut off. We just scraped over
Shap after being stopped at Oxenholme.
I had a spell firing as the engine slipped
and struggled as we breasted the summit at
walking pace. The driver had also had a go
on the shovel. The pressure was down to

180 lbs, and we ran down to Carlisle with both injectors on for a long time as the water level in the boiler had become very low.

We were an hour late away from Carlisle and had the assistance of a banker over Beattock. During this leg of the journey both the baffle plate and the protector ring fell into the fire and melted, adding to the dross on the firebars. We arrived at Glasgow at 10.55 p.m. I was very black and tired after nine and a half hours and four hundred miles on the footplate. I was assured that this had been an unusually bad run.

I returned to Euston the next evening on the 9.25 p.m. in the cab of English Electric diesel 10001, which had doubled headed the thirteen-coach train with 10000. We went up Beattock at forty-five miles per hour and came down the other side at eighty. The brakes were twice as slow as on a steam locomotive, both in application and release. The fumes and lack of action also made me sleepy, but we arrived at Euston twenty minutes early.

BELOW
The author drove 75078 on the return leg of his driving test in 1959.

RIGHT
Blue Peter, A2 No. 60532, turned out to be a disappointment for the author because of technical problems.

Finally, a trip on the Great Eastern, thanks to Mr R H N Hardy, whom I had met while firing to Bert Hooker of locomotive exchange fame. It was 1958, diesels were being introduced on this region in increasing numbers. I joined Stratford men on "Britannia" "Pacific" 70040 Clive of India at the head of ten coaches on the down 'Norfolkman' with one stop at Ipswich and then Norwich. The pressure soon dropped from 240 lbs down to 200 and we had a rough time to Ipswich with water in the bottom of the glass. While we were stopped the fireman got her round a bit and he kept 200 on the clock to Norwich and we arrived right on time. At 2.40 p.m. I rejoined the crew who had turned the engine and worked on the fire. We had five coaches on to Ely where the load was made up to ten coaches. I fired this return trip but overloaded the fire on the climb out of Cambridge, and I began to sweat as the pressure dropped to 200 lbs. A slightly lighter fire improved

matters considerably and we had 220 lbs the rest of the way, arriving at Liverpool Street two minutes early. The ride was harsh for a "Pacific", and noisy. The crew were ready to 'go for it' when they could, making it an interesting and lively experience for me. Later, Mr Hardy quizzed me on what I had learned while in possession of the footplate pass he had issued to me. Back at Nine Elms main line trains were still being hauled by the elderly "King Arthur"s and "Lord Nelson" 4-6-0s. One foggy day in February 1959, having worked "N15" 30784 to Southampton Docks, my driver suggested a tour around the works at Eastleigh which were handy to the loco shed in which we stabled our engine. We saw a "Lord Nelson" being fitted with a new copper firebox. In contrast, three "West Country"s (Braunton was one of them) were being rebuilt to conventional style, and five "Merchant Navy"s were next in line. The rebuilt Bulleid "Pacific"s often appeared on the Sunday

10.54 a.m. Waterloo to Bournemouth, smelling strongly of paint. Gone were the days of a twenty minute oil round, now it took an hour and a quarter to do three sets of Walschaerts valve gear and a bit of climbing up the high running plate to attend to other oilboxes. To my eye they looked better and the cabs were cooler with less hot pipework, and we could now see where we were going! Instead of having to throw out fifty square feet of fire with a long shovel (having first taken off the cab doors) we could now drop the clinker into a hopper ash pan and then into the pit. They rode harder than before because their springs were less flexible, and they had a tendency to develop a 'knock' at about thirty-five thousand miles. The resulting thumps and bangs made them seem reluctant gallopers until they were travelling at more than sixty miles per hour.

However, gallop they could! On 26th March 1959, driver Len Rickard and I were in charge of rebuilt "Merchant Navy" No. 35017 Belgian Marine hauling the 11.05 a.m. non stop to Salisbury with a thirteen-coach train. We did the 83.8 miles in 77 minutes with a top speed of around 102 miles per hour down the bank from Grately. During those 77 minutes, three thousand gallons of water were used, and I shovelled about two tons of coal through the firehole door.

On 22nd May 1959 I took my driving test on "Lord Nelson" No. 30851 Sir Francis Drake. We had a good run, 10.54 a.m. out of Waterloo and right on time to Basingstoke. A pint in the Railway Arms, then back to London on 75078. Inspector Pemberton got off at Woking and told me that I had passed. None of Len Rickard's firemen had ever failed. I was twenty-three years old and steam had just another eight years left before it ended on the Southern in 1967. During that period the number of steam locomotives working on the Southern declined from about 1200 to about 150, twenty-four of which were based at Nine Elms. The "Merchant Navy"'s had all been rebuilt by the end of 1959, and of the pre-war Southern designs only Maunsell's "S15"'s, a few 2-6-0s and 0-6-0s remained by the end of 1965. By 1966 we had just begun to become aware of the emptiness of the shed. In the 'autumn of steam' the 'leaves' fell so slowly that when I look today at photographs of the period I cannot remember that it looked so run down and empty.

In August 1966 "A2" No. 60532 Blue Peter arrived from Scotland for an LCB special to Exeter. On Sunday the 14th I was booked to drive it as far as Salisbury. Although I had been looking forward to the trip from the start it did not go well. Because of a broken rail in the dip under the coal hopper we had trouble getting off shed on time. When the engine was warm enough to shut the cylinder cocks the middle set stayed open - but we had to go! My fireman, C Collier, did his best, but a tender full of Welsh dust did not suit the engine at all. We only had a nine coach load and ought to have romped away. Several signal checks on the way to Basingstoke and an easy schedule masked the situation at first, but from Worting we were limping along with a dead fire and the centre cylinder cock still blowing hard. We had used 3000 gallons of water already and went over Grately with 100 lbs on the gauge and only a quarter of a glass of water. Black with dust and soaked in sweat we could only roll down the hill to Salisbury while we filled up the boiler. The crew that took over for the run to Exeter stopped for lack of steam on Honiton bank,

BELOW
Driver Len Rickard standing in front of 'Merchant Navy' No. 35005 Canadian Pacific, before leaving London with the Bournemouth Belle. In her rebuilt form, Canadian Pacific was saved from the scrapard and is still at work today.

they had one well to get that far. A North Eastern fireman had ridden with us; both he and I had tried our hands at firing but to no better effect. It had been a disappointing experience for I knew what she should have been capable of having fired "A3"s "A4"s and "A1"s to Bill Hoole on the Newcastle trips.

Looking at my logbooks for those final years when we represented the last main line steam line in Britain, I can see patterns that I had not noticed at the time. Duff trips and tough trips are recorded, then a note that said "We have been clearing out the old coal off the ground around the 'triangle'". Old coal, mostly dust with some earth and weeds, its calorific content leached out by sun and rain. This was what my firemen were having to use when they made up the firebed prior to running light engine to Waterloo. Sometimes, while I was oiling up the engine, my mate in the cab would be struggling to find some lumpy coal to shovel. Two spare firemen, ankle deep in the dust in the tender, searched by hand for pieces of coal to throw to my fireman for his fire. It is on record that young Nine Elms drivers 'tore about a bit' in the final months of steam. Some of them were followed about night and day by enthusiasts that yearned to 'clock a ton'. The track had been re-laid for 90 mph plus running for the new electric services. Those last days when every platform end held a throng of photographers will never be repeated. We were just doing our daily job. Steam locomotives today are operated as an 'out of the ordinary' event.

When the final steam engine left its train to run back to the shed and its crew went home, the crowds left the platforms and they did not bother to watch trains for the next ten years.

Chapter Fifteen
Epilogue

Despite the best efforts of the 'modernisers' the history of steam does not end in 1968. Sent to the scrapyards in their hundreds many engines died under the cutter's torch. I remember watching No. 35004 Cunard White Star being sliced vertically like a piece of cake at Eastleigh depot. My mate and I had walked to the shed in driving rain after working the 5.30 p.m. down from Waterloo on 7th February 1967. Four days later, on the same turn, I picked up the severed regulator handle from where it had dropped on the ground and carried it with me on the return working to London.

Two hundred dead engines lay in Barry Island. Pilgrimages were made to see them as reverently as the 'faithful' are wont to do for 'saintly relics'. Driver Alan Wilton of Nine Elms moved heaven and earth to

LEFT
One of the many engines sent to Barry Island for scrap. However, all were saved, as the last engine was removed for restoration in the 1980s.

preserve an un-rebuilt "West Country" No. 34023 Blackmoor Vale. Groups of enthusiasts began to organise themselves so they could purchase their own locomotives with the starry-eyed intention of returning them to steam. It was totally irrational, but today, almost forty years later, the results can be seen as proof that time cannot destroy that which has been constructed, only lack of interest can destroy these things.

The Duke of Gloucester has been rescued and reconstructed by a group who were fascinated by its unique qualities. They have made her a more reliable performer in the process. On 1st June 1988, I sat in the spotless cab of rebuilt "Merchant Navy" No. 35027 Port Line. She had been restored in just five short years from a Barry wreck by a two hundred strong group who had raised £120,000 and learned many new skills in the process. I placed my hand on the warm regulator and felt an instant sense of empathy with the huge machine. It had been twenty-one years since I had last placed my hand on that regulator at the head of the 5.30 p.m. Waterloo to Bournemouth in July 1967. With my fireman, Vic Spillett, we had maintained a steady eighty miles per hour during the journey. A new "A2" "Pacific" is under construction as I write, and a new generation is falling under the spell of the iron horse.

The history of steam is still being made.

BELOW
The Duke of Gloucester has been skilfully rebuilt and, with many other preserved engines, is keeping the age of steam alive.

Part Two

Introduction to Three Famous Men of Steam

RIGHT
A portrait of Robert Stephenson.

In this section of the book I enlarge on the lives and careers of three of the famous men of steam. Some of the events that are recounted have been touched on elsewhere in this book. I have defined their qualities roughly as follows: George Stephenson can be called a visionary and the prophet of the steam railway system. Samuel Smiles, who wrote the contemporaneous account of George Stephenson's life, is his St Paul. George could do no wrong in his eyes. Robert Stephenson excelled as an accomplished chief of staff, motivating and freely acknowledging the input of those who worked for him. Isambard Kingdom Brunel created a railway of heroic proportions stamping it with a style that forever made the Great Western different to all others. He was no locomotive engineer, however, but his enthusiasm for the propulsion of large ships by steam power enables me to include him among the heroes of steam.

The accounts that follow are old and familiar stories to students of railway history. It is important to remind ourselves how very different the world was when these men were creating the railway system that our modern trains still use. The following accounts will illustrate what I mean. For instance, in 1832, George Stephenson was heavily criticised for bringing in his own men instead of using local workmen. Traditionally, the stagecoach proprietors would recruit stagecoach drivers from men that were local to each stretch of the road between towns and villages. They would best know the road and how to manage the horses over it.

Stephenson was creating his new iron road by the labour of outsiders, itinerant gangs of navvies who had expertise in the building of cuttings, tunnels and embankments because of their experience in canal building. None but the men of Northumberland had any knowledge of the management of his iron horses. So it was the Geordies from the pit railways that were recruited to be the first locomotive drivers, shedmasters and firemen. It was a monopoly, but it was the result of the paucity of experience in this field.

And again, when we casually read

MAIN
Stephenson's locomotive Rocket in her later, modified form.

that Robert Stephenson and Co. built a locomotive and delivered it to work on such and such railway, we should contemplate the fact that the boiler and wheels were lifted onto a horse-drawn lorry which took them to a wharf, where they were placed on the deck of a wooden sailing vessel that then carried them to Liverpool (or Maidenhead, in the case of North Star) to be put on rails for the first time when the tracks had reached the point of disembarkation.

We should also think of the extreme youth of men like Daniel Gooch, locomotive superintendent of the Great Western at twenty-one. Having designed some efficient and speedy engines for his railway, he often drove them himself. When the Great Western first reached Exeter, Gooch drove a special train which left London at 07.30 a.m. and was hauled by Aetaeon a loco with seven foot driving wheels. The train reached Exeter (194 miles) at 12.30 p.m. After attending a celebratory dinner, Gooch was back at the controls of his engine, setting off again at 5.20 p.m. He reached Paddington at 10.00 p.m. Gooch had driven 387 miles, had been at the engine shed long before 07.00 a.m., had only sat down at the dinner and had probably drunk several toasts to the success of the line before driving the return journey. It was almost certainly a 19-hour day, with 18 of them on his feet. For this reason enclosed cabs were not thought a wise option even by the regular drivers who feared that comfort would induce drowsiness.

The young Gooch was driving over newly created lines. No-one "knew the road", as we twentieth century drivers did having observed or fired scores of times over a route before signing for it. We see the result of this, on 30th September 1852. Gooch was at the controls of Lord of the Isles on the directors' special from London to Birmingham. The train was made up of 10 coaches, only one of which had a brake (and a guard), and this was next to the engine. The 120 mile run was to take two and three quarter hours. None of the men on Lord of the Isles knew the road. At Aynho they saw a stop signal at danger, thought it was a distant or warning signal and drove past it. Before they could stop they ran into the back of a mixed goods and passenger train that was shunting in the station! Luckily the driver of the mixed train, having detected the sound of wheels on the line behind him, hastily put on steam to get away from the approaching train. The sudden jerk that was the result broke a coupling on his train and some coaches and wagons were left behind, into which the special smashed. Lord of the Isles was derailed, wagons and coaches splintered and some platform stone work was torn up.

The other driver's alert action had prevented serious injuries to passengers and crew, but the board of trade was critical of everyone. Trains did not get failsafe continuous brakes for another twenty-three years.

Finally, to put us all firmly into that young and carefree age of the new iron road, when North Star ran the first train from Paddington to Maidenhead in June 1838, the return trip, after a celebratory dinner, was proceeding at an average speed of thirty miles per hour when Bristol director, T R Guppy, walked the full length of the train on the tops of the carriages. This was the world in which the heroics of George, Robert and Isambard were displayed. Times are very different today, though young men are still as daft.

Chapter Sixteen

George Stephenson Visionary

George Stephenson was born on 9th June 1781 in the lower room at the west end of a four-roomed house situated a hundred yards from Wylam, a colliery village on the north bank of the Tyne. He was the second of six children. The house stood by the side of the old post road between Hexham and Newcastle, and was divided so that four families had one room each. The rooms had bare rafters above, unplastered walls and clay floors at ground level. A wooden tramway along which chaldrons were hauled by horses ran in front of the house, and young children had to be watched lest they were run over.

George's father, Robert, was of Scottish descent. He had been living at Walbottle while working as a labourer at Wylam colliery, but when he met and married Mabel Carr and was made fireman of the old pumping engine that served the mine, he had moved to the house at Wylam. 'Old Bob' was a friendly man and 'Bob's Engine Fire' was a place where village children gathered to hear the stories that he told and to watch the wild birds that also found him hospitable. Robins hopped at his feet for a crumb or two, and George grew up with a similar affection for birds.

Eight years later, when the coal ran out, George's father found a job at Dewly Burn colliery, and the family moved to a one-roomed cottage by a stream next to the mine.

BELOW
Before the advent of the steam engine, coal was brought out of the mines by men and horses.

The young George earned a few pennies to help the family finances by watching over Widow Ainslie's cows that grazed along the wagon ways. Using clay from Dewly bog, he and a pal, Bill Thirlwall, made model engines using twine and corks to make the 'pit machinery'. Both of them were future engineers, Bill later became the engineer at a mine near Alnwick. As George grew older he also earned pennies for leading ploughing horses, but he was always keen to work at the colliery. He started by picking slate out of the coal and later progressed to management of the gin horse that wound the haulage rope at the mineshaft. In time he became his father's assistant, firing the engine at Dewly. He was fourteen and earned a shilling a day. When the coal ran out again the family moved home, settling in another one-roomed cottage in Jolly's Close near Newburn. When the Newburn mine was enlarged, George became a fireman himself at the age of fifteen, working twelve hour shifts for two years sharing the duties with a lad named Coe. Now George's ambition was to be an engineman, and to that end he studied his engine so that when another new pit opened at Water Row, between the Wylam wagon way and the river Tyne, he joined his fireman father, and at the age of seventeen he took the job of engineman or 'plugman'. He was now paid more than 'Old Bob' and

P.

was responsible for the proper working of the engine as it drew water up from the mine workings. When the water level fell suction holes were exposed preventing the pump from 'drawing'. These holes had to be plugged by the 'plugman' so that suction could recommence. As engineer he was required to call on the chief engineer in cases of the machinery malfunctioning, but as a result of his genuine interest in the engine he gained a good understanding of its parts and he was able to fix most breakdowns himself.

The working of a Newcomen engine was accompanied by an extraordinary amount of wheezing, sighing, creaking and bumping. When the pump descended there was heard a plunge, a heavy sigh, and a loud bump. As the pump rose and the suction took effect there was a creak, a wheeze, another bump and a rush of water as it was lifted and poured out. We can picture the eighteen year old at the place of his work watching the swift glide and swing of the huge pumping engine. Every click and thump told a story, and the sudden rush of water as it welled up spoke of the hundred thousand gallons pumped during each twelve hour shift.

George could not yet read, but he was of a

George Stephenson Visionary

steady and thoughtful nature and if he could get someone to read an old newspaper to him he learned of the exploits of Bonaparte, then at large with his armies in Europe. From time to time information on the wonderful engines made by Boulton and Watt would form a short item of news, and he realised that only by 'learning his letters' would he be able to improve his knowledge.

As a grown man he had the courage to attend classes in the village with the sons of colliers and labourers, three evenings a week for threepence, paid to a poor schoolteacher named Robin Cowens. In 1799 he attended Andrew Robertson's arithmetic classes in Newburn for fourpence a week, doing his homework while attending to his pumping engine at the colliery.

At Water Row he learned the art of braking an engine. This was a well paid job, and it was thanks to his pal Coe that he was given the chance to acquire the skill.

Subsequently he was given the brakesman's job at Black Callertons Dolly Pit in 1801 at the age of twenty. He now lived in the house of a local farmer and became the admirer of Fanny Henderson, a servant at the house. Fanny was comely, sweet tempered, modest and sensible, and George, who now mended shoes to add to his income, was delighted to have her small footwear to work on from time to time during the nightshifts at the colliery when there was less for him to do.

Some months later he was offered the brakesman's job at Willington Ballast Hill for higher pay. This encouraged him to set up home with Fanny in a rented cottage at Willington Quay. With the help of Fanny's savings added to his own he furnished the cottage, and in November 1802 they were married in Newburn church. Their cottage was one of several that lined the riverside, behind which was a huge hill of ballast taken from the holds of ships

LEFT
One of Stephenson's achievements still in use, the power wheel used to drive a lathe at Killingworth Colliery, Northumberland.

NEXT PAGE
Invicta, built by Rober Stephenson & Co. for the Canterbury and Whitstable Railway, 1830.

about to be loaded with coal. George was to be brakesman of the stationary engine that hauled the wagons of ballast to the summit of the great pile. As a result of his studies, George was able to sign his name in the church register. After the ceremony the couple visited the home of George's parents, 'Old Bob' was still a fireman but was becoming infirm. Then, while seated on a farm horse with Fanny behind him and her arms around his waist, they rode the fifteen miles to their cottage. The bridesman and bridesmaid, similarly mounted on a second horse, accompanied them.

George still used his spare time to add to his savings. He worked at shovelling ballast out of the ships' holds and made and repaired shoes. After a chimney fire that sooted up their prized eight day clock, he cleaned and repaired it so successfully that he also became the local repairer of clocks and watches. It was at Willington Quay that George's only son, Robert, was born on 18th October 1803.

Towards the end of 1804, George was persuaded to take the job of brakesman at the West Moor Colliery at Killingworth, which had vast coal reserves and employed large numbers of people. The move was shortly marked by tragedy when Fanny died of consumption, leaving George with his baby son. While grieving for his lost companion he was asked to superintend the working of one of Boulton and Watt's engines at a large spinning works at Montrose in Scotland.

He left Robert in the care of his sister, Elender, and, with his kit on his back, walked the two hundred miles to Montrose. Stephenson stayed in Scotland for about twelve months and was paid enough to enable him to save twenty-eight pounds.

George Stephenson Visionary

During his time at Montrose he solved the problem of excessive wear on the bore and leathers of the pumping engine that he was responsible for. The wear was caused by sand carried in the water flow. George's solution was a twelve foot deep wooden 'boot' that he placed in the sump at the lower end of the pump. The water then spilled into the sump leaving the sand behind. His return to Killingworth was again made on foot.

During his absence George's father had been scalded in the face and blinded by an accident at the engine house. George used fifteen pounds of his savings to settle his father's debts, and he arranged for his parents to move to a cottage at Killingworth, where he supported them for many years. Although Stephenson was again employed as a brakesman, this was a low point in his life. England was at war, taxes were high, trade was bad and men were being pressed into serving the Navy or militia. In order to avoid military service George spent the remainder of his savings, plus six pounds that he borrowed, to pay for a man to serve in his place. He was too poor at this stage to emigrate to America as his sister, Anne, and her husband had done.

His fortunes began to improve again in 1808 when he was contracted to be one of three enginemen supervising two engines at the West Moor pit. The engines worked night and day and two of the three enginemen were on duty at any time, each of them earning about twenty shillings per week. George made some alterations to the winding gear which increased the life of the haulage ropes. His habitual regular examination and maintenance of his engine and the knowledge that he acquired of the function of each part, gave him the chance

to make a name for himself as a 'fixer of sick engines'. In 1810 the Newcomen engine at the newly opened Killingworth High pit failed to reduce water levels even after twelve months of pumping. Stephenson had not been impressed by the design of the engine when he had watched it being erected, and as the months passed and still the mine was unworkable he put his mind to the problem. After a thorough investigation of the engine he offered to make it work in a week. After having been given permission to try his hand, George did as he had promised. Choosing his own workmen he took the engine apart. He enlarged the water injection cock and ensured that it shut quickly and completely when the piston stroke began. He also raised the water cistern by ten feet and increased the boiler pressure from 5 lbs to 10 lbs. These alterations took three days to complete. Then, in front of a large crowd of observers, the engine was started with a series of exuberant bangs which caused some alarm. Once under load, however, the engine settled down and began to lift water. At ten o'clock that night the water in the pit had begun to fall, and by the next afternoon the workmen were able to descend to the bottom of the shaft. As a result of this achievement George was appointed engineman at the Killingworth High pit at a good wage, plus a payment of ten pounds for repairing the engine. By 1812 he was engine wright at the pit with a salary of one hundred pounds per year, and a horse to ride while making colliery inspections.

Stephenson continued to educate himself. He had a friend by the name of John Wigham who was a farmer's son, and who gave him instruction in mathematics. He would set problems on George's slate for him to work on during his shifts. Wigham also taught George to draw plans and sections. When George became a famous man he remained grateful to the farmer's son who had helped him in his efforts to gain knowledge.

His own son, Robert, now nine years old, was a bright lad and was interested in the engines that George managed. For his part, George was determined that Robert would not have to face life unable to read or understand the use and rules of mathematics. In his spare time George made extra money from clock repairing and shoe making. He also devised patterns that enabled women to cut out and make their own clothes. He used this extra income to send Robert to school at Long Benton then, when the boy was twelve, to a school in Newcastle. He bought the boy a donkey on which he would ride to and from school, wearing a grey suit that George had cut out and made, and with his books and food for the day on his back.

At home George taught his son how to read a plan of a machine without having to rely on textual information to describe the machine's action. At the pit, George set up engines above and below ground thus reducing the number of horses working underground from a hundred to fifteen. The time was approaching when George would apply his skills to locomotive construction. The old wooden wagon way that had been laid between Wylam and Lemington village had been replaced in 1808 by a plateway of cast iron enabling a single horse to draw up to three full wagons. In 1812 a rack had been laid along the plateway allowing Blackett's second primitive combination of Trevithick's and Blenkinsop's designs of travelling engine to be tried out. The maker, Tommy Waters of Gateshead, on finding it would not move, held down the

safety valve and declared that: "Either he or she would go." The engine moved briefly before it 'flew all to pieces', Tommy was fortunate to survive. A third engine, also with rack drive, proved to be more successful and could pull eight or nine loaded wagons - when it did not jump off the rack.

Later the rack was taken away and William Hedley's smooth tyred engine appeared on the plateway after it had been re-laid with heavier rails. Stephenson went to see the engine that was working daily to and fro past the cottage in which he had been born, and came to the conclusion that he could make an engine that would work more steadily

and efficiently. In 1813 George suggested to Lord Ravensworth, principal partner of the lessees of Killingworth colliery, that he might construct a travelling engine to haul coal from the mine to the river.

George was given permission and funds by Lord Ravensworth, whom some called a fool for advancing money for such a project. It took ten months to build the engine which ran for the first time on 25th July 1814. It could haul eight loaded wagons totalling thirty tons up a slight gradient at four miles an hour. It closely resembled the Blenkinsop locomotive except that spur wheels driven by two cylinders engaged with gearing

LEFT & BELOW
A miner works while another looks on with a safety lamp, the workings of which are shown below.

that turned smooth tyred wheels along the rail head. A chamber around the chimney preheated the water that was delivered to the boiler by a feed pump. The engine had no springs, but an attempt was made to equalise the weight between the boiler unit and the coal and water carrier by a lever connection.

It took a lot of effort to create this cumbersome and clumsy machine. George had to instruct the workmen and sort out initial problems with John Thirlwall, who was the blacksmith at West Moor. The spur gears did not provide a smooth drive and soon the teeth became worn and

jerky in operation. At the end of twelve months the engine proved to be no more economical than horse power had been.

George saw that the major problem was the use of spur gearing. The following year he took out a patent, dated 28th February 1815, for an engine with direct drive from the pistons to the wheels. He used a ball and socket joint at the crossheads and crankpins to allow for uneven track causing a varied lift to the axles. At first the driving wheel sets were united by rods that joined cranks fitted to the axles at right angles to each other, but the cranks fractured in use. He then resorted

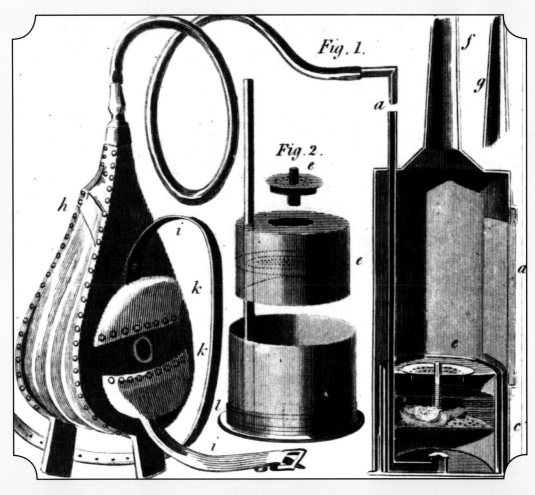

George Stephenson Visionary

to a chain running around indented wheels on the axles, so that the wheels turned in unison and maintained the right angle setting of the driven cranks, one to the other.

Eventually he hit upon a better method. The wheels on each side were kept in unison by rods on the outside of the wheel, so there was no need for a cranked axle. Direct connection to the crankpins was the elegant solution, and one still used on modern locomotives. Exhaust steam from the cylinders was turned into the chimney to speed up the rising action of the smoke. The coke fires burned more brightly as a result.

There was one more innovation that George tried on his improved engine in 1816. The light plateway responded badly to the increased weight and traffic, the rail joints became uneven so that derailments and slipping occurred too often, and at that time Stephenson was unable to get springs made that would support the heavy weight of the engine. His solution was to build four small cylinders into the lower part of the boiler, the pistons of which bore on the axles. Boiler steam on the upper side of the pistons enabled each piston to take a quarter of the weight of the engine. The weight was then equal on each wheel despite changes in rail level. He also improved the design of the chairs that supported the track so that the rail ends met on more level terms.

It was about this time that George was risking his life in gas filled mine workings to test a safety lamp that he had invented. Explosive gases came out of the coal seams and miners using candles to see their way were often killed in underground explosions. The lamp that Stephenson developed became known as the 'Geordie Lamp' and though Stephenson did not fully understand the

'science' of what he had made, he knew that it was 'safe' when he himself took it into explosive gases. Sir Humphrey Davy is famous for his safety lamp which he developed in accordance with scientific principles that he knew and understood. The coal owners presented Sir Humphrey Davy with £2000, and Stephenson was given a hundred guineas. A certain amount of argument relating to the priority of their concepts was inevitable. Stephenson's supporters raised a further £1000 for George.

Locomotive building continued when Stephenson was asked to make a steam operated line between Hetton colliery in Durham and the coal shipment wharf on the river Wear, near Sunderland. The line was to be eight miles long and, because of the steepness of the gradients en route, there were five self acting inclines (i.e. full wagons going down hauling empty wagons going up) and two inclines with fixed engines hauling wagons by rope. Five of Stephenson's iron horses worked the remainder. The railway opened on 18th November 1822 with George's brother, Robert, acting as resident engineer.

George's son, Robert, had left his Newcastle school in 1819 and was apprenticed to the head viewer at Killingworth for three years, after which George paid for him to attend Edinburgh University from October to the following summer. The six months cost George £80.00. He was now a married man again as in 1820, after many years alone, he wedded Elizabeth Hindmarsh, a farmer's daughter from Black Callerton.

Although George's engines continued to work their regular duties over several colliery lines year on year, the general public had yet to learn the potential value of rail transport. In the south of England, investors had lost money when the first public railway had been laid between the Thames at Wandsworth Creek and Croydon. Known as the Surrey Iron Railway it began life in 1801 with a track length of twenty-six miles. Worked by horses or donkeys the line failed to make a profit, despite an income from charges levied on the public for moving their own goods.

Nearly twenty years later a second but more famous public railway, the Stockton and Darlington, was created largely through the efforts of a group of Quaker businessmen led by Edward Pease of Darlington. The initial plan had been for a horse-drawn tramway, but in 1821 Mr Pease had been visited at his home by Nicholas Wood, viewer at Killingworth and George Stephenson, the engine wright.

With the help of his more eloquent companion, George made a successful application to become the engineer of the proposed line. He also extolled the virtues of his steam engines. Mr Pease visited Killingworth, had a ride on an engine and, not only did he get George appointed to the post but also obtained an alteration to

LEFT
Portrait of the
civil engineer
Joseph Locke.

the Stockton and Darlington act of 1821, so that in 1823 it allowed the use of steam engines to haul goods and passengers over the line. Edward Pease also agreed to invest in Stephenson's plan to build a 'locomotive manufactory' in Newcastle. George put up the one thousand pounds that had been presented to him for his miners' safety lamp.

Assisted by his son, Robert, as chainman, George made his preliminary survey, and the gauge was settled at four foot eight and a half inches. Wrought or malleable iron rail imported from Sweden was his preferred choice, but some use had to be made of cast iron rails initially for reason of economy. Work commenced on the line in 1822, and the locomotive works was set up to build engines by 1824, with Robert at the drawing board. Three of Stephenson's engines were ordered for the new railway. However Robert, who had obtained a position as a mining engineer in Colombia, left England and the newly opened locomotive works in June of that year, and set sail for South America. George had made him undergo a medical examination of some intensity before he left, probably hoping to prevent his son's departure, but, medical notwithstanding, off he went on a three year contract at the age of twenty-one. He left his father to cope with a self imposed workload that became heavier every year that his son was absent. Determined to be recognised as the man most suitable for each and every post that called for an engineer with experience in the new technology of railways, on 25th May 1824 George had secured the appointment as engineer to the proposed Liverpool and Manchester Railway just a month before Robert departed. So it was that George was deprived of his son's emotional and practical

help at a time when the completion of the Stockton and Darlington was in sight, and his humiliation before the committee considering the Liverpool and Manchester bill in March 1825 was yet to come.

Through the efforts of his father Robert had been provided with a useful theoretical and practical training in engineering. In 1821 he had assisted the superintending of the construction of the Hetton Railway. He had taken part in the initial survey of the Stockton and Darlington, and had assisted Mr William James with his survey of the proposed Liverpool and Manchester Railway. The following year he had assisted George with the working survey of the Stockton and Darlington, and in 1823 he helped to set up the locomotive works at Newcastle. In the early part of 1824 Robert had completed designs for a stationary engine for the S & D rope hauled incline at Brusselton. This wealth of experience had made Robert a prime target for the 'head hunters' of the day, desperate for engineers for the mines of South America.

George Stephenson replaced Mr James as surveyor of the Liverpool and Manchester when that gentleman suffered imprisonment for debt. By this time, George had superintended the construction of nine railways and had built fifty-five engines, of which sixteen were steam locomotives. Mr James had faced relentless opposition and obstruction to his work from the landowners and those with coaching and canal interests. Stephenson and his assistants fared no better, and his plans and estimates proved to be imperfect. Some had been done in haste, others had been done by moonlight. His assessment of the costs did not accord with works as shown in the plans, but were

RIGHT
British statesman William Huskisson who was killed at the opening of the Liverpool and Manchester Railway.

sometimes based on a later solution that had not yet been included. Against the advice of the L & M directors George failed to hide his enthusiasm for the use of steam locomotives on the line. He often mentioned potentially alarming speeds of above four or five miles an hour in his replies to questions. Also, there was not an established engineer he could call on who would support his intention to build the railway across Chat Moss and run steam locomotives over it. Chat Moss was such a waterlogged and unstable bog that in 1821 Mr James, having sunk into it with his theodolite, could only save himself by laying down and rolling himself to firmer ground and the helping hands of Robert Stephenson.

Although the preamble was passed by one vote, the Bill to make the railway was rejected by the Commons committee and was withdrawn by its promoters. The enquiry had lasted more than two months. Stephenson was seriously depressed, not only by the lost opportunities but also because during the enquiry another engineer, William Cubitt, had been called by the L & M directors to correct George's estimates. One of his young surveyors, Hugh Steele, later committed suicide in Stephenson's office.

Despite his low spirits Stephenson had continued to build steam locomotives, and four months later Locomotion No. 1 was completed at the Stephenson company works in Newcastle, in time to haul a party of directors on a trial run from Shildon to Darlington on 26th September 1825. George was present while his brother, James, drove the engine. Locomotion weighed about six and a half tons. It had a wrought iron boiler with a single flue from the firebrick lined furnace. This single tube did not transmit enough heat into the water to avoid the occasional red hot chimney. It was fitted with two cylinders with each one let into the boiler top in line with an axle. The pistons transmitted their power to the relevant wheel via parallel beams and long connecting rod to the crank pins. Coupling rods kept the back and front wheels in phase, and to ensure reliable starting (no dead centres) the crank pins on the rear wheels were ninety degrees behind those on the leading wheels. For this reason, the coupling rod pins on the rear wheels were on return cranks. No springs were fitted though three point suspension was provided which would have improved traction. A four wheeled tender carried 240 gallons of water and 15 cwt of coal.

On Tuesday, 27th September 1825 the Stockton and Darlington Railway officially opened. At 06.00 a.m. the directors watched Robert Stephenson's stationary engine at Brusselton as it lifted a train of wagons up an incline more than a mile in length in just seven and a half minutes. Eight minutes later the wagons were at the foot of the opposite incline where Locomotion No.1, driven by George Stephenson, waited for the wagons to be added to his train. Coupled to his engine were six wagons loaded with coals or flour, then there was a coach for the directors and proprietors, next there were twenty-one empty coal wagons crowded with passengers and lastly the six wagons of coal from the incline.

When George started the train it was preceded by a horseman carrying a flag. On reaching a favourable gradient George told the rider to get out of the way, and Locomotion and her train carried on to Darlington reaching speeds of up to fifteen miles an hour on the way. The train carried 453 people and weighed 93 tons. On the

return journey 600 people rode in the train, some of the loaded coal wagons having been replaced by empties. On less favourable gradients the twelve mile journey took three hours. However, the time probably flew by as they carried a band of musicians, and the route was lined with onlookers and riders on horseback. Everyone had been given a holiday for the occasion. A dinner at the Town Hall in Stockton ended a long and triumphant day for George and his friends.

Initially 'travelling engines' were not the primary source of motive power on the S & D. The public had access to the railway and horse-drawn traffic predominated, and the steepest gradients were operated by fixed stationary engines. Stephenson's first passenger coach constructed in October 1825 and named Experiment, was also horse-drawn, and horse-drawn coaches could cover twelve miles in sixty minutes. The general 'cut and thrust' up and down such a shared system eventually forced the proprietors of the Railway to take over the running of the line themselves.

In the meantime, undaunted by the failure of their first Bill, the L & M directors planned a second application for the 1826 Parliamentary session. George was replaced by Messrs George and John Rennie, engineers, and Charles Vignoles to survey and plan the line. The use of steam locomotives did not feature in this Bill, and to minimise the destruction of roads and houses it was proposed that Liverpool would be entered via a tunnel, which also avoided some obstructive private estates. The Bill was passed on this occasion and George was soon reappointed as engineer to carry out the work, his first priority being to cross Chat Moss. Work began in 1826 and initial attempts appeared

to be a great waste of time and materials, as everything sunk without trace into the depths of the bog. In Newcastle, George's preoccupation with Chat Moss meant that Timothy Hackworth at Shildon had to turn the new locomotives and their drivers into reliable performers. L T C Rolt writes "...Hackworth was the world's first shedmaster..." and Shildon men were to take their expertise around the world. It was also the partial cause of his locomotive company running into financial difficulties, to the consternation of Edward Pease. Subsequently Pease contacted Robert in Colombia urging to return home, which he did in 1827. After four years, during which time it had often seemed that the twelve square mile bog could never bear a railway track let alone the weight of a train, Stephenson's methods ultimately proved to be successful. Against all contemporary engineering opinion he had laid down a floating bed of hurdles made from branches and stuffed with dried heather. These were then topped with fine stone, over which the track was laid. Chat Moss was conquered and the railway was completed on 1st January 1830.

Much of the rest of the line had been completed before 1830, major works included a mile and a half long tunnel into Liverpool and the 100 foot deep cutting made through rock at Mount Olive. Stephenson's preference for steam hauled trains was not shared by other professional engineers, and the L & M directors were divided by conflicting advice. However, in 1828 Stephenson was allowed to build a locomotive that was used during the final stage of the line's completion. A decision was made that engine builders should be given the chance to demonstrate the

BELOW
Pumps draining the Kilsby Tunnel of quick sand during construction of the London - Birmingham Railway.

efficiency and suitability of their machines at a public trial to be held in October 1829 over a section of the line already laid at Rainhill. A prize of £500.00 was offered.

Stephenson's Newcastle works produced Rocket, a 'racy' looking four wheeled engine designed by Robert Stephenson and Henry Booth. It was a major departure from the heavy 'Killingworth colliery' style. It had large (4' 8") single driving wheels and small trailing wheels. The boiler was only six feet long but it had twenty-five three inch diameter flue tubes between its water jacketed external fire box and the tall chimney. Two inclined cylinders drove crankpins on the driving wheels, and exhaust steam aided the combustion process by being released up the chimney. A four wheeled tender carrying fuel and water was attached. The multiple tube innovation had been suggested by Henry Booth.

The trials attracted thousands of onlookers. Each engine had to complete ten trips travelling at a minimum speed of ten miles per hour over a short section of the line. After some attention to the engine a further ten trips were to be completed. There were two other competing machines, one being Timothy Hackworth's Sans Pareil, an old fashioned four coupled engine with a return flue boiler. It had two vertical cylinders the exhaust from which was piped up the chimney, and was sharpened by constriction of the pipe end. The other engine was Novelty, a light machine more akin to a road carriage than a locomotive. It had a horizontal and vertical boiler and a vertical piston driving the wheels through a bell

crank. Bellows were provided to stimulate the fire. Novelty was built by Messrs Braithwaite and Ericsson. Rocket successfully performed all the required tests and reached a top speed of twenty-nine miles an hour. Robert Stephenson and Henry Booth shared the £500.00 prize money. Novelty, which had reached thirty miles an hour, set light to her bellows and was forced to retire. Although too heavy for the four wheeled class Sans Pareil was allowed to run, but broke down during the trials as she was unable to maintain water feed to the boiler. Also, Sans Pareil's fuel consumption was unduly high because the design of the sharpened exhaust blast caused a considerable portion of her fire to be ejected up the chimney.

It was as a result of the Rainhill trials that the steam locomotive came to eventually replace the horse. During the twelve month period between September 1829 and September 1830, Robert Stephenson continued to improve the basic design of each subsequent engine turned out of the works. With the eighth engine Northumbrian which had a separate smokebox the Rocket type had fully evolved from its Killingworth ancestors.

The Liverpool and Manchester Railway was officially opened on 15th September 1830 when the most modern engine, Northumbrian, driven by George Stephenson, pulled out of Liverpool with the first of eight trains conveying a total of six hundred people. Robert drove No. 6 Phoenix, George's older brother, also Robert, drove No. 7 North Star. No. 1 Rocket was driven by Joseph Locke, No. 5 Dart was driven by Thomas Gooch, William Alleard drove No. 3 Comet, Frederick Swanwick drove No. 4 Arrow and Anthony Harding drove No. 2 Meteor.

The special trains used both tracks and during the stop for water at Parkway, the Duke of Wellington's train, drawn by Northumbrian, waited to be passed by other trains. The pro-railway and pro-steam MP William Huskisson was unfortunately run over by Rocket as he attempted to scramble up into the Duke's train. George Stephenson had the injured and dying man lifted aboard Northumbrian, which was unhooked to speed off for medical help at Eccles. George worked his engine up to thirty-six miles an hour during that desperate journey, though in later life he was to express his opinion that train speeds should be kept to forty miles an hour. He warned that metals could fracture under the strains involved, and one wonders if his appreciation of this danger had lurked unpleasantly at the back of his mind during the dash for help in 1830. Mr Huskisson died that night of his injuries.

During the next three months Stephenson's engines hauled fifty thousand passengers sharing 954 runs between Liverpool and Manchester. At the age of 49 George was vindicated in his steadfast advocation of the travelling steam engine. His services as supervising engineer were sought on all sides as business men of the day formed companies to connect their towns by rail. He also retained an interest and talent for mining. George had recommended that Robert, then 27, be retained as engineer of a sixteen mile railway between Leicester and a coal producing area near Swannington. While surveying the line Robert realised that coal deposits were to be found near Ashby-de-la-Zouch, below Snibston. The new railway would earn money by moving coal, the land above it was for sale. George and some of his Liverpool friends purchased the estate

NEXT PAGE
A platform at Eustion Station, terminus of the London and Birmingham Railway. 1837.

in 1831 and after some determined digging and the exercise of George's mechanical expertise, the coal layer was finally reached in 1832. In order to be near the work George had moved from Liverpool to make a home at Alton Grange. He created a village at the mine with houses, schools, church and chapel for the miners and their families.

The promoters of the London and Birmingham Railway had sought Stephenson's advice in 1830 with regard to the route the line should take. There were the usual difficulties with landowners and horse breeders in 1832. The Railway's promoters had to triple the money they offered to buy the land they needed, so that in 1833 a reintroduced Bill was passed by both Commons and Lords committees. On George's advice Robert, who had married Frances Sanderson in 1829, was made chief engineer of the L & B at a salary of £1500.00 per annum. Although the construction of this one hundred and twelve mile railway demanded great civil engineering skills, the line was completed in 1838.

The years between 1834 and 1837 were the busiest of George's life. During this period he covered twenty thousand miles by post chaise from Alton Grange. He visited Ireland and Scotland, and made journeys to his London office that was opened in 1836. He was engaged as engineer on the North Midland Railway, from Derby to Leeds and opened in 1840; the Normanton and York, opened 1840; the Manchester and Leeds, opened 1840; the Birmingham and Derby, opened 1839 and the Sheffield to Rotherham, opened 1839. He also advised on railway construction in Europe. In 1835 King Leopold of Belgium made George a Knight of the Order of Leopold at a public

ceremony honouring the 'father of railways'. Never at ease with letter writing, George sometimes dictated to his secretary as many as thirty-seven letters a day, and on one occasion for twelve hours continuously. In 1838 he was engaged on the Chester to Holyhead survey, and in 1841 he moved his home for the final time to Tapton House, near Chesterfield Green. Once again he was using his mining talents. He made a pit at Clay Cross to extract coal and at Ambergate he developed a quarry to make lime.

Locomotives constructed at the Stephensons' company works were sold to a worldwide market. Adaptations of the innovative Patentee design of 1834 were the basis of the most successful locomotives on broad or standard gauge throughout the world. The fifteen year 'Battle of the Gauges', during which speeds of over seventy miles an hour were recorded, was eventually settled in favour of Stephenson's four foot eight and a half inch Standard Gauge, which he had stipulated for the Stockton and Darlington. In 1842 George was working on an idea he had for a self braking system suitable for higher speeds.

The 'Railway Mania' of 1845 resulted in an extraordinary change in attitude with regard to railway building. The battles George had fought to gain acceptance for his concepts of railway and steam locomotion were a thing of the past, everybody wanted to invest in even the most crazy schemes. Between 1844 and 1846 440 railway acts were passed by the House of Commons, and more than £180 million pounds of new railway capital was authorised. A complete reversal of the land owners' attitude to railways had taken place, George was besieged in his son's London office by speculators

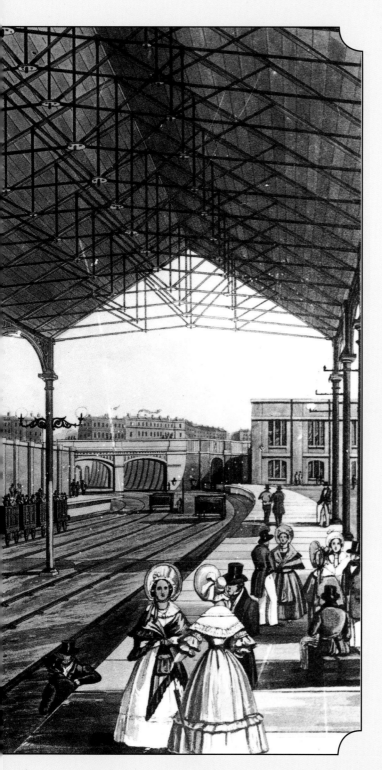

that wanted his name on a prospectus.

George was also an honoured visitor to Belgium, and in August 1845 he reported on the proposed route of the West Flanders Railway. As early as 1835 he and Robert had been asked by King Leopold for advice on the construction of a railway system that would open up the ports to the vast reserves of coal and minerals within the country. In 1837, when the line between Brussels and Ghent was opened, George and his party were the honoured guests at the ceremonies, processions, dinners and public ball which celebrated the occasion.

In September 1845 George travelled to Spain to examine the route of the proposed Royal North of Spain Railway. He was taking time out from the supervision of his Clay Cross collieries, having agreed to a six week absence while being paid for his expenses only. After many long days of surveying from dawn to dusk, sometimes sleeping the night on dirt floors, George advised Sir Joshua Walmsley that the terrain was difficult and that the expected level of traffic could not justify investment unless land, labour (convicts) and timber were provided to the company. They waited ten days for a decision from the Spanish government, but as no such decision was forthcoming, Walmsley withdrew his offer. The railway company was later dissolved.

George returned to England, travelling almost continually day and night, determined to arrive by the 30th November. The strain that he had put himself under had weakened him and he was seen to be ill when the group reached Paris. During the voyage from Havre to Southampton he developed pleurisy and they had to bleed him. Once at home, George recovered gradually, but

George Stephenson Visionary

he was a weakened man after that trip.

In 1847 George was a guest of Prime Minister Sir Robert Peel at his mansion at Drayton Manor. He made a speech contrasting the change in attitudes of land owners towards railways between 1825 and 1847. He also took a crack at Brunel's determination to do everything differently. George derided the Great Western's broad gauge engines with the boiler on one carriage and the engine on another, the ten foot wheels which were supposed to go at 100 miles per hour, the steep gradients and the atmospheric system. "Our North Star engine was called upon to carry the traffic. It did double duty, though engines, like horses, need a rest." Perhaps Sir Robert flushed as he heard this as he had supported many of those ideas.

In 1848, while keeping an eye on his colliery interests, George enjoyed his life at Tapton House. He involved himself in horticulture and farming, and indulged in his boyhood interests in the study of birds and animals. On 26th July 1848 he visited the Mechanics Institute at Birmingham to read his paper on the 'Fallacies of the Rotatary Engine'. However it seemed that his lungs had never regained their health and, back at Tapton, bouts of fever culminated in a massive haemorrhage of his lungs which finally killed him on 12th August 1848, at the age of sixty-seven.

He was buried at Trinity Church, Chesterfield. A statue that had been commissioned by the boards of the Liverpool and Manchester and Grand Junction Railway companies two years previously, arrived from Rome shortly after his death and was placed in St George's Hall, Liverpool. A second statue was put in the original and very imposing Great Hall of Euston Station.

MAIN
George Stephenson's first successful steam engine, the property of Hetton Colliery, takes part in a centenary rocession, 1925.

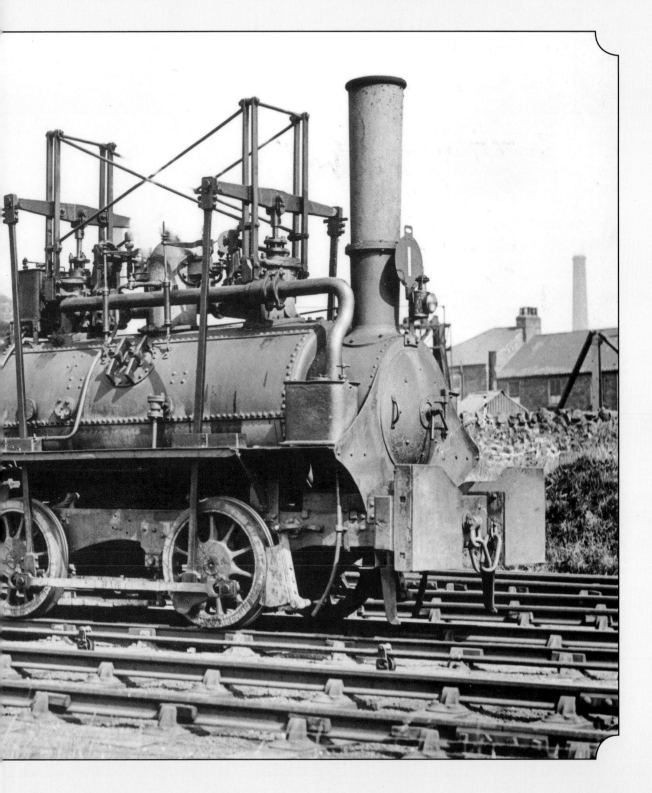

Chapter Seventeen

Robert Stephenson Grand Overseer

A large and sensitive portrait of the Stephensons hangs in the Institute of Civil Engineers, Great George Street, London. To a life-long locomotive man like myself it arouses something of the awe and affection that churchgoers feel when they contemplate a religious icon. After all it depicts the prophet of the steam locomotive, the father of a clan of enginemen that would spread worldwide from harsh Northumbrian roots. By his side the son that improved and developed the older man's concepts. I have a copy of the painting in my library.

The Stephensons are often referred to as 'Messrs Stephenson'. It is difficult to write of one man without getting entangled in the activities of the other. Their lives and achievements form a complex pattern, a pattern that is the result of George's systematic way of tackling his problems. We see it demonstrated in accounts of George's early work to improve the efficiencies of pumping engines, and later in his retirement years when he applied his mind to the production of the perfect cucumber! Just like a prize winning vegetable from his father's greenhouse, George's son was 'shaped' by early and appropriate training in order to develop the skills and knowledge most beneficial to his father's business.

Robert learned mining skills as an apprentice to Nicholas Wood at West Moors. Surveying skills were developed while helping his father on the Hetton Colliery project. In 1822 he had assisted William James for twelve months with his survey of the Liverpool and Manchester Railway. He also assisted George with the Stockton and Darlington survey, even deputising for the older man during Parliamentary appearances when he was only eighteen years of age.

The education that George gave to his son forged a 'key' to the doors that had been closed to him by his own lack of formal schooling. To the quick, intuitive observance of the father was added the son's growing ability to refine, explain and develop ideas that formed in George's canny mind. Only once did Robert depart from this role, when he took a brief 'holiday' from 1824 to 1827 in South America.

On 23rd June 1823 at just twenty years of age, Robert had been made the managing partner of the locomotive and engine building works, "Robert Stephenson and Company". As we have seen, this was a partnership between the Quakers, Edward Pease and Michael Longdon, and George and Robert Stephenson. Robert had just returned to Newcastle after a short spell at Edinburgh

RIGHT
George Stephenson and his son Robert at work together in their cottage, circa 1820.

University. Pease loaned him £500 for the purchase of shares, and Robert was made responsible for setting up production and engaging workmen. For this he was paid a salary of £200 per annum. In 1823 both George and Robert travelled extensively, visiting London, Bristol, parts of Shropshire and even Ireland in the hunt for orders to be fulfilled at the Newcastle works.

In April 1824 Robert once again visited London to see the Stockton and Darlington Act through Parliament. It appears that at this time he became acquainted with Fanny Sanderson, the daughter of a city merchant. In May, just as he was completing drawings of the stationary engine for the Brusselton incline, he was offered a contract to re-open gold and silver mines in South America for the Colombian Mining Association of London. For some

time experienced engineers had been 'head hunted' for such schemes. Some ten years earlier Richard Trevithick had sailed to Peru to mine for gold, though no-one had heard from him since!

To Robert it must have appeared that there was a fortune to be made by using his skills as a miner, a surveyor and a steam engineer. Perhaps he thought that Mr Sanderson would look with favour upon a young man who had made himself some money by his own enterprise. Perhaps he just wanted adventure and some freedom from a controlling parent and those bossy Quakers? Whatever his reasons, Robert was sufficiently tempted by the offer to declare to his partners that he would only be away for twelve months when he had in fact signed a three year contract.

Robert carefully prepared for his new project by having some surveying instruments made to his order. George, who was busy in Liverpool working on the foundations of the Liverpool and Manchester Railway, arranged that Michael Longdon would take over Robert's duties for the twelve months his son would be abroad. Robert travelled from London to Liverpool in a dangerously overloaded stagecoach, where he said goodbye to his father on the quay side.

Robert set sail on 8th June 1824. The name of the ship, Sir William Congreve was rather more appropriate than at first apparent. Well known for his invention of the clock with the zigzag rolling ball escapement which also bears his name, Sir William Congreve was at the time far more famous for his rocket propelled ordnance. Fired from especially adapted ships or from land from a sort of tripod, these rockets had a range of some two miles and proved to be very effective against the French in the later stages of the Napoleonic wars. They were also used against the Americans in 1812. While being very effective against an enemy, Congreve rockets were also prone to premature explosion and were no doubt highly dangerous. One writer, alarmed at the potential speed of George's steam locomotives, warned that "to travel at twice the speed of a stagecoach would be as ridiculous ... as being fired off in one of Congreve's ricochet-rockets", no doubt reasoning that both inventions 'phizzed' loudly. It surely follows that the sardonic Geordie humour of the Stephensons caused them to name their most famous engine Rocket.

The so-called roads of Colombia were more like bridleways along and up which mules carried everything. Everything including Robert and his small party which set out on a 1200 mile trek from Caracas to Santa Fe de Bogota, the capital of Colombia in the foothills of the Eastern Cordillera, to meet the commercial manager of the Mining Association. He continued on to the area of operation at the ancient Spanish City of Maniquita, where the completely overgrown and abandoned mines were located. At every step he was hindered by false information from guides who promised rich deposits of ore which seldom materialised. The local authorities had to be treated to extravagant social gatherings, and trouble frequently broke out between the rowdy Cornish miners and their North country engineer in charge.

Although Robert had, with his uncle Robert in February and March of 1824, taken the trouble to visit Cornish mines to familiarise himself with their working methods before leaving England, this did not impress the Cornish miners. Often drunk, they derided his abilities and refused to take his orders. His warning letters to the Mining Association in London were ignored, and heavy equipment continued to arrive, only to be piled up alongside the narrow mule paths that flanked the River Magdalena. He suffered fever and depression and, although he had eventually set up a house on the eastern slopes of the Andes where the temperatures were a reasonable 75°, he keenly felt the lack of a decent library and well equipped laboratory. Letters from England told him of lost orders at Robert Stephenson and Co. due to bad workmanship, and that his father was under attack for the botched survey of the Liverpool and Manchester Railway. Edward Pease wanted out of the partnership but George could not afford to buy his share. All in all it was a sorry state of affairs and, to cap it all by 1826 the South American mining speculations also began to fail.

The Mining Association tried to get George to give his permission for Robert to stay a while longer, at least until a successor could be found. But father and son had both had enough, and in June 1827 Robert made the return voyage via New York, arriving in Liverpool in November that year to meet the white haired George, now 46 years old. On his way, Robert had chanced to meet the destitute Richard Trevithick and was able to loan him the £50 he needed for a passage back to England.

The South American 'adventure' taught Robert several lessons which ultimately hardened him until he was able to present a steely eye to those who failed to meet with his expectations. However, away from his professional career, the young engineer was often lonely and depressed, surrounded by the malign forces of nature and duplicitous mankind. It is possible that he sought the comfort of narcotics at this time. In later life he was advised by friends to cut down on his habit. He was often 'hipped'. Those great and tireless men who died young may have depended heavily on substances that were more acceptable in the early nineteenth century than they became in the twentieth.

Be that as it may, his competent presence back in Newcastle brought a swift improvement to the fortune and reputation of the Robert Stephenson and Co. locomotive works. The primitive Killingworth engines were supplanted and the prize winning design of No. 1 Rocket had, by loco No. 8 Northumbrian, begun to develop into the modern locomotive with its separate smokebox and cylinders almost parallel with the ground.

Further improvements followed. The Planet had a cranked driving axle and inside cylinders beneath the smokebox. The Patentee had a set of wheels behind the driving wheels to support a large firebox, and it was this design of 1834 which really set a worldwide standard for locomotive design at the time. In 1837 R S & Co.'s 150th engine North Star became No. 1 to the fledgling Great Western Railway. It was a most efficient engine and one which Daniel Gooch was to use as the basis for some very successful broad gauge locomotives.

In 1842 Robert Stephenson adopted and patented the link motion invented by one of his pattern makers, William Howe. For the first time the expansive use of steam was possible and engine No. 71 could be reversed in the dark by any driver. To avoid paying patent dues, Daniel Gooch of the Great Western Railway made his own version of Stephenson's link motion by substituting a fixed link and fitting a radius rod that could be raised or lowered.

In the same year Robert decided to lengthen the boilers of his engines from 9 feet to 13 feet in order to reduce the working temperature of their smokeboxes, and to avoid the problem of their chimneys becoming red hot. By 1846 150 engines of his 'long boiler' patent were in use, though they were found to be mainly suited to freight work due to their instability at speed. The inventive William Howe produced a scheme for a three cylindered engine with three sets of valve gear, which Stephenson patented as a Stephenson-Howe design.

Concurrently with the improvements he was making to his locomotives, Robert was also involved with various civil engineering activities. Among other projects, he attended to the Canterbury and Whitstable Railway and, in 1829, the sixteen mile Leicester and Swannington Railway. He joined the Institute of Civil Engineers, and he and George were appointed joint engineers of the London and Birmingham Railway. By this time George had recovered from the humiliation he had suffered for the poor survey of the Liverpool and Manchester Railway. In January 1830 he had the deep satisfaction of driving Rocket over the 'uncrossable' Chat Moss. However, George's finest talents did not lie in the day to day organisation of major works and on 14th June 1830, the 26 year old Robert was left in sole charge of the London to Birmingham survey. From 1833 Robert battled to complete the L & B, which was eventually achieved after a

RIGHT
The stationary engine chimneys and locomotive engine house near Camden Town on the London and Birmingham Railway line, 1840.

MAIN
The famous Doric arch that marked the entrance to the London and Birmingham Railway's Euston, Terminus.

further five years, during which time Robert estimated that he had walked the 112 mile length of the line no fewer than fifteen times.

It was an incredible display of his ability to overcome the many problems inherent in such an undertaking. The route was divided into thirty sections, for which individual contractors agreed on a price and completion date. Sometimes the geological make up of the ridges through which they had to cut or tunnel delayed progress. Costs could mount beyond initial estimates and it was not uncommon for contractors to find themselves bankrupted.

Robert was obliged to complete seven of the sections using railway company labour in order to keep to his timetable. Especially trying were the works at Tring which required long cuttings some 60 feet deep; Kilsby, where thirteen pumping engines (at George's suggestion) removed 2,000 gallons of water every minute for eight months to dry the quicksands that were inundating the tunnel bores. Other particularly difficult sections of the line included Wolverton, Blisworth, Rugby and Coventry.

Although Robert missed the target date of January 1838, the line was officially opened in September that year. He rode the open footplate of the Directors' special during the inaugural run from London to Birmingham, where he and fellow dignitaries later dined at Dee's Royal Hotel.

The Directors appointed Robert Engineer-in-Chief of the London to Birmingham line, at a salary of £1,500 per annum. He had proved himself to be a great civil engineer, achieving independence from his father while adding lustre to the name of their railway construction company, George Stephenson and Son. Clients from abroad

LEFT
Scottish engineer
James Naismith and
his patented steam
hammer.

now honoured them and sought their advice.

By 1840 Robert was a wealthy man living a comfortable life at his home at Haverstock Hill with Fanny, his wife of eleven years. His achievements were suddenly and brutally turned to ashes when Fanny was diagnosed with cancer. Two years later she died. They had no children.

As though this personal tragedy was not enough, Robert was also being hounded by creditors of the failed Stanhope and Tyne Railway. He had accepted shares in the railway in lieu of his fee for acting as consulting engineer in 1832. However, the company was not incorporated and as it could no longer pay its debts the creditors turned to the shareholders for redress. Robert's wealth made him a prime target and his liabilities were potentially unlimited. It was a very nasty situation, though he eventually managed to sort it out by organising the formation of an incorporated company which took over the Stanhope and Tyne under the name of Pontop and South Shields Railway Company. Robert did not risk buying shares in any subsequent railway scheme, and those shares he had he sold before the great crash of railway stocks.

Any remaining liabilities were covered when George Hudson's Newcastle and Darlington Junction Railway made use of the path of the Pontop and South Shields in order to at last unite London with Newcastle in 1844. George Stephenson, who had always promoted such a link with London, and Robert were in Hudson's 'Grand Opening Train' on 18th June 1844. There was the inevitable banquet, and workers from Robert Stephenson and Co. paraded through the town waving banners.

Robert's next great works were to be the bridges and viaducts required in order to lay routes to the north of Newcastle that had been selected by George to construct a line to Berwick and Edinburgh.

Unlike George, Robert was diffident about taking all the credit for these great works. He had probably learned the hard way that Hubris precedes Nemesis in the affairs of engineers as surely as they did in the affairs of Greek heroes. As a result, when he made a bad mistake, as he did with the Dee Bridge at Chester which collapsed under a train in 1847, damage to his reputation was less than it might have been had fellow professionals harboured spiteful feelings towards him.

Throughout his career he had confided his attacks of self doubt to others, especially when facing unexpected geological or engineering difficulties. He often sought the help of brother engineers and gave his support in return when asked for it. His responsibilities had mushroomed with George's semi-retirement after 1840, and must have given him many a sleepless night. At one point he was attending to thirty-three different new schemes.

On 6th October 1846, the first piles for his high level rail and road bridge between Gateshead and Newcastle station, were driven in at the rate of thirty-two feet in four minutes by Naismith's newly invented steam hammer. This hammer had also been invaluable in the construction of Brunel's huge iron ships. Opened in August 1849 the bridge spanned 515 feet of river and a ravine that had many buildings clinging to its steep slopes.

A graceful twenty-eight arch viaduct over the Tweed at Berwick was completed in 1847. For the Chester to Holyhead line (surveyed by George in 1838)

Robert Stephenson Grand Overseer

Robert designed his famous Conway and Britannia bridges, the foundation stones for which were laid in 1846.

In order to create spans of great strength and at navigable heights, Robert enlisted the expertise of William Fairburn, a shipbuilder at Millwall and a one time work mate of his father in his coal pit days. The rectangular tubes of wrought iron were riveted together on the banks of the river. At Conway, two 400 foot tubes, each 1,180 tons in weight. For the Britannia bridge two tubes 1,524 feet long, each weighing 1,600 tons with 450 tons of rivets in each tube.

MAIN
The Menai Suspension Bridge, designed by Thomas Telford, and the Britannia Tubular Bridge, designed by Robert Stephenson, between mainland Wales and Anglesey.

The tubes were floated into position under a scheme devised by Mr Evans who was contracted to build the bridge at Conway. In order to position the tube laden pontoons Robert relied on the skills of Captain Claxton, who directed sailors used to managing ropes, cables and capstans in a manner that no landlubber could equal.

Claxton had also been of great assistance to Brunel when his steam ship Great Eastern had stuck fast at Dundrum Bay. Now Brunel and his Captain were with Robert as he prepared to battle with tides and winds to position those great tubes. Present among the many spectators was a very frail George Stephenson, who had but four months more

to live. By April 1848 the first 400 foot tube was in place to be raised cautiously by hydraulic rams. The second tube was installed by January of the following year.

The Britannia Bridge at Anglesey was similarly erected, and was officially opened on 18th March 1850 when three locomotives hauled a 500 ton train through the completed tube. The second tube and its track were completed in October 1851. Robert also designed tubular bridges for the Alexandria and Cairo Railway in Egypt and in 1853 acted as engineer in chief for the construction of the Victoria Bridge in Canada. This 6,588 tubular bridge crossed the St Lawrence River at Montreal. Work started in April 1854 but the bridge was not to be completed until 24th November 1859, shortly after Robert's death.

During the final years of his life Robert discovered the missing element that released him from lonely responsibility. He did not marry again and he remained childless. The steam yacht Titania became the love of his life, on board which he spent many weeks at sea in the company of friends. He had the first Titania built in 1850 but it was destroyed by fire at Cowes in 1852. His second Titania was bigger at 184 tons and had a large saloon library. He loved reading and

collecting fine art. A final voyage to northern England took him to visit his childhood haunts on the Tyne, and to the scene of his most recent effort at Holyhead. With winter approaching he sailed to Egypt in October 1858, eventually meeting up with Brunel, who was accompanied by his wife and son Henry. They shared Christmas dinner at the Hotel D'Orient. At the time, both men were suffering from a chronic nephritis known as 'Bright's disease'. By February 1859 Robert was back in London. In the summer of that year he suffered poor health, yet still managed to sail to Norway in the autumn to attend a banquet held in celebration of the completion of another new railway. It was during this banquet that Robert's health took a sudden turn for the worse and he returned to England with some haste. The following month, October 1859, Robert Stephenson died at his home in Gloucester Square. His death was widely mourned, and the funeral cortege travelled through Hyde Park to Westminster Abbey where his body was placed in the nave next to the grave of another great engineer, Sir Thomas Telford. On the great rivers of Thames, Tyne, Wear and Tees all shipping lay silent with their flags at half mast. The 1,500 employees of Robert Stephenson and Co. marched to a memorial service in the church of St Nicholas in Newcastle. One of his pallbearers was Joseph Locke, who had succeeded him as President of the Institute of Civil Engineers.

Chapter Eighteen

Brunel the Heroic Engineer

Brunel was undoubtedly a visionary, he wrote of his tendency to build castles in the air. He was also a great Chief of Staff and could inspire the perfect team to drive forward the most complex projects. He was certainly a hero who showed great bravery facing physical dangers and in facing the responsibilities that resulted from attributes one and two above. His engineering and architectural constructions were heroic in their scale and grandeur. His final battle and early death at the age of fifty-three calls to mind the story of Captain Mahab's fatal pursuit of the leviathan in Herman Melville's Moby Dick. His final creation, the SS Great Eastern, had originally been called 'Leviathan' and the last photograph of Brunel standing bareheaded before its funnel is as tragic as the image of Captain Mahab inextricably caught up and doomed by his obsession with the great white whale.

One cannot help warming to Brunel as a human being. Visionaries like George Stephenson can be prickly characters who are jealous of their status as formulators of unarguable truths. A man like Robert Stephenson who was shaped by his father to fulfil a role, who having lost his wife, committed himself to a childless and work-centred life, somehow lacks the appeal of a Victorian family man such as Brunel. Eighteen Duke Street was both Brunel's office and his source of relaxation. It was his home from the day of his marriage to the day he died, with his family around him.

Two hundred years ago on 9th May 1806, Isambard Kingdom Brunel was born at Portsmouth. His father, Marc Isambard Brunel, was an engineer from France. His mother, Sophia Kingdom, although English was living in France when she met Marc. Brunel senior had a talent for invention which had been successfully used to increase the production of ships' rigging blocks for the British Royal Navy. As a young man he had met Sophia in Rouen while serving as an officer in the French Navy. Unsympathetic to the revolution he had moved to America in 1793 where he worked as a surveyor and engineer. Later he was granted American citizenship and he became the chief engineer for New York. He moved to England in 1799 in order to put his inventive genius at the service of the Navy administration. Sophia, who had been imprisoned by the French from the start of their hostilities with England,

RIGHT
Isambard Kingdom Brunel's steamship the 'Great Eastern' was launched in 1858.

eventually managed to return to London in 1795. She began corresponding with Marc while he was in America and they married when he returned to England in 1799.

The outline above is brief, but illustrates the very cosmopolitan and romantic background from which our third engineer, Isambard, emerged. He father was a creative engineer with an affinity for naval matters. Isambard's unrelenting tendency to reject the conventional approach may also stem from this background, as does his final enthusiastic involvement in the building of large steam powered ships.

Like Robert, his early education was organised by his father so as to make best use of his inborn talents. From an early age he was good at mathematics and was interested in surveying. At home the family were hosts to notable men of science. Marc was elected to the Royal Society in 1814. Babbage, Faraday and Sir Humphrey Davy were his friends. From the age of eight Isambard studied at Dr Morrell's boarding school in Hove. In 1820 he continued his education in France at Caen College and at the Lycee Henri IV in Paris. The Lycee specialised in science and mathematics. He then began an apprenticeship with Breguet et Fils of Paris, the foremost watch and clockmaker of France.

It was while he was at Breguet that his father's various enterprises foundered, largely as a result of too much invention and not enough attention to business matters. Marc and Sophia were arrested in 1821 and interned in the King's Bench debtors' prison, Southwark. By August 1821 Marc's influential friends, who included the Duke of Wellington, succeeded in getting overdue money out of the Treasury to pay off his

debts. This was moneys owed to Marc for Government contracts. Marc and Sophia returned home and in August 1822 the sixteen year old Isambard came back from France to work in his father's office.

At this point we might usefully compare the life experiences of Robert and Isambard. We know that they will meet and become friends. At age 16 sixteen Robert, who had hardly known his mother, had been brought up by his father in a rough Northumbrian mining community. His education was sketchy, he had been a coal pit apprentice at the same age that Isambard had emerged from a comprehensive science based education in France to experience the rarefied company of notable scientists of the day. As a result, I K Brunel did not exhibit the single minded loyalty to the steam locomotive that Robert had imbibed while at his father's side.

For instance, Isambard and his father wasted ten years and £15,000 of Marc's money trying to develop the 'GAZ' engine, which was based on the theories of Davy and Faraday. Some time later Isambard again wasted much time and money on another rival to the steam engine, Clegg and Samuda's atmospheric railway system of 1838. Despite these aberrations, I.K Brunel's inclusion in this book is appropriate due to the perfection of his railway engineering and also to mark his enterprise and courage in the building of ocean going ships driven by huge steam engines of his design.

In 1825 the Brunels began their great battle to drive a tunnel beneath the Thames from Rotherhithe to Wapping. Marc had invented and patented a rectangular tunnelling shield with thirty-six work places for the miners. The shield was pushed against the tunnel face by screws acting against the

Brunel the Heroic Engineer

brickwork behind it. A brick width of earth was shovelled away, the frame was levered forward, and a new brick course was put in behind it. By this means the frame would move forward about a foot each day.

There had been two earlier attempts to tunnel under the Thames, Marc's shield was designed to cope with the unstable subsoil that had ruined those initial forays. However, it was soon clear that the conditions of the subsoil were even worse than had been allowed for. Despite this, by 1827 350 feet of tunnel had been completed, then Marc fell ill, his resident engineer resigned and Isambard was appointed in his place. At the age of twenty- one he displayed great

courage and energy. On one occasion he spent five continuous days underground, sleeping when he could on the planking erected for spoil collection. When the tunnel roof gave way he had himself lowered in a diving bell suspended from a boat so as to find the weak point in the river bed. When the tunnel flooded again, he and three others rowed themselves to the site of the break in the flooded tunnel to examine the bank of mud that had poured through the shield. He was badly injured by a heavy fall through a manhole in the works yard in October, but still took his place at a banquet held in the completed section of the tunnel a month later. The next year he was nearly

drowned when water again broke in while he was underground, the ill effects from which kept him away for several months. In 1828, due to the financial difficulties of the tunnel company, work on the tunnel ceased and the face was bricked up. The tunnel was not to be finally completed until 1843. Part of Isambard's convalescence had been spent in Bristol at Clifton. When he learned of a competition to design a bridge that could span the Avon gorge he submitted four out of the twenty- two entries for consideration. Eventually, in 1831, his design for a suspension bridge was accepted. Work

started in August that year, but riots in Bristol prevented progress which, together with some financial difficulties, meant the bridge was not completed until 1864. However, in 1836, while the stonework was being constructed, a one inch bar was drawn across the Avon gorge between the two towers. The bar was installed to enable material to be transported from one side of the gorge to the other, but a fault developed. Isambard, then thirty years of age, rectified the problem while suspended over the 230 foot drop in a basket.

In 1829, when his near contemporary,

BELOW
The Great Western Railway's Temple Meads Station in Bristol designed by Isambard Kingdom Brunel.

Robert Stephenson, was fully occupied with the production of steam locomotives for the Liverpool and Manchester Railway and many other young engineers were making names for themselves, Isambard felt himself to be in the doldrums. He had tried for the post of engineer to the Newcastle and Carlisle Railway and again as engineer to the Birmingham and Bristol Railway. He had well connected friends and had himself been elected a member of the Royal Society in 1830, but still he lacked an appointment that would establish his credentials.

However, in 1833 his fortunes began to improve. The merchants of Bristol had decided that they needed a railway to connect their port to London in order to compete with the rival port of Liverpool. Initially they were unable to attract sufficient financial backing, but gained further support in 1832 and by 1833 were in a position to look for an engineer. Charles Babbage recommended Isambard, who was duly appointed. The Great West Road and the stage coaches that travelled on it had a new rival, The Great Western Railway Company.

Isambard began his survey of the line, spending many hours out of the twenty-four at the task. In 1834 he gave evidence before the House of Commons Committee for eleven days. The Royal assent for the full line was granted in 1835, and he began to set out the 117 mile route, avoiding gradients and severe curves that might limit the speed of trains travelling over his new railway.

George Stephenson's 4 foot 8 1/2 inch track gauge had been rejected by Isambard in favour of a broad 7 foot gauge that would allow lower centres of gravity, wider fireboxes and larger cylinders to be built into the locomotives that would haul the trains.

It is doubtful that any of Stephenson's ideas could have been uncritically accepted by this young engineer, who had listened from childhood to the table talk of men of science like his father's friend, Sir Humphrey Davy.

In receipt of a £2,000 annual salary, Isambard was able to set up a rather grand house at 18 Duke Street, overlooking St James' Park. The following year he married Mary Horsley whom he had known since 1832.

In less than six years, the line to Bristol was opened throughout its whole length. It had been divided into nine sections and the work had proceeded from both ends. Not only had Isambard rejected Stephenson's gauge but he also rejected the length of the rails, the shape of the rails and the way they were supported. Three foot five inch rail lengths, held by chairs on stone blocks had been suitable for the Liverpool and Manchester. The GWR was laid with fifteen foot bridge rails fixed directly to longitudinal timbers having cross members and piles at fifteen foot centres. This proved to be a mistake. Though the ride was firm and the rails minimally stressed, it was difficult to prevent settlement of the timbers between the piles. Soon the first twenty-two miles of the track had to be altered to prevent the piles from propping up the timber-borne rail ends, which then imparted a 'see-sawing' motion to the trains.

At this stage, Brunel almost lost the confidence of some of the Great Western Railway board of directors. The Liverpool contingent was of the opinion that Brunel should seek the advice of the Stephensons. As we have seen, Brunel's locomotives were inadequate for their task, and in 1840 Daniel Gooch had been given a free hand to produce his own designs.

Brunel the Heroic Engineer

Nevertheless, the railway that Brunel went on to create was magnificently proportioned, endowed as it was with impressive earthworks, viaducts and elegant bridges. The stations at Bristol Temple Meads and Bath had Tudor style hammer beam detail that enhanced the beauty of an unbuttressed over all roof. The second Paddington Station replaced the temporary building of 1838, and was built in 1854 and included the Great Western (Royal) Hotel. In this case, Isambard's station roof was after Joseph Paxton's design for the Crystal Palace built for the Great Exhibition of 1851. The hotel, by P C Hardwick, was in the style of a French chateau.

At Box Hill, which stood in the way of the line six miles west of Chippenham, Isambard excavated a 9,600 foot tunnel on a falling gradient of one in a hundred towards its

LEFT
The western entrance to Box Tunnel, designed by Brunel, on the Great Western Railway.

RIGHT
The wooden paddle steamer Great Western, designed by Isambard Kingdom Brunel, is caught in a severe gale, 1846.

western end. Eight shafts were sunk to enable digging to proceed, the maximum depth was about 300 feet. The strata that lay within the hill had been checked by sinking smaller 'test' shafts. The tunnelling began in 1838 but the work was sometimes halted by flooding, however the line generally advanced by about six feet per day. A thousand men worked in shifts around the clock, though a hundred of these would lose their lives before the tunnel was completed in 1841. The face of the excavation was thirty-six feet high and thirty feet wide, and the tunnel was left unlined where it passed through hard rock. A ton of gunpowder was used every week to blast through the rock face. And this was only the first of the eight tunnels that he had to build between Chippenham and Bristol.

One of the most notable aspects of Isambard's personality was his ability to direct his energies to more than one project. Far from being content at his sudden change of fortune in 1835, when at one moment

he despaired of ever making a name for himself, then at the next he was appointed engineer in charge of the Great Western Railway, he subsequently set himself an even greater challenge by proposing to continue his transport system across the Atlantic to the shores of America. As a result of this proposal, made at a GWR meeting in August 1835, the 205 foot keel of the longest ship in the world was laid at a Bristol shipyard the following June.

The Great Western paddle steamer was Isambard's concept of a link between nations, where passengers could travel via the Great Western Railway from London to Bristol, and from there to the USA by the company's steamship. Despite the ongoing problems at Box Tunnel, Isambard applied himself to the design of the massive pair of steam engines that would drive the twin paddles of the SS Great Western. It was to be the biggest marine engine that had ever been built, though its working pressure was only 5 lbs

Brunel the Heroic Engineer

per square inch. Brunel was assisted by the expertise of Captain Claxton, a retired naval officer, and T P Guppy, the Bristol Railway director, who were both members of the building committee. By July 1837 she was launched, and in April 1838 made the passage to New York in eighteen days, returning in fourteen days. The 500 ton American sailing ships which had dominated the Atlantic trade now had a speedier rival. SS Great Western.

carried on to make sixty-seven crossings in eight years, and was eventually broken up in 1857 after twenty years of service.

The simultaneous conjunction of his enterprises continued. In July 1839 he began the construction of his second ship the SS Great Britain, a 3,500 ton iron hulled steamer with screw propulsion. Its 15,000 horsepower engines, designed by Isambard, were arranged to drive a propeller shaft longitudinally.

BELOW
The Royal Albert Bridge, under construction.

Four cylinders in pairs at 60° drove an over head crankshaft with an eighteen foot wheel that was partially visible within a skylighted housing above deck. Toothed chains around the great wheel rotated a smaller wheel on the propeller shaft. This ship was completed in July 1843. The merchants of Bristol had good reason to be delighted by the energy of their young engineering genius. Not only had he connected them with London, but concurrently provided a potentially rapid connection with New York and created plenty of jobs for the workmen of their city. Unfortunately for Bristol, however, the dock company failed to enlarge its locks as they had promised, and once launched the ship had to be based at the rival port of Liverpool. Brunel's third ship, the Great Eastern, would be built in London. In the meantime, Brunel had an idea which he thought would speed up trains over the hilly terrain in South Devon.

Around the time that Isambard's Great Britain was being fitted out, he was trying to solve the problem of how to run a fast train service over the undulating route that had been chosen between Exeter to Plymouth. The line from Bristol to Exeter had been completed in 1844 and there were now 194 miles of track over which Daniel Gooch's Firefly engines made good speed from London. However, between Newton Abbott and Plymouth gradient of between 1 in 41 and 1 in 64 existed in at least ten places. Brunel judged that locomotive-hauled trains would be badly affected. He became interested in an idea patented by Messrs Clegg and Samuda and demonstrated in 1840 on a short length of track at Wormwood Scrubs. It was known as the atmospheric system, and it did away with the need for a locomotive.

A cast iron pipe with a continuous slot in the top was laid between the tracks. The slot was made airtight by a greased leather flap. Stationary steam engines were erected at intervals along the line to pump air out of the pipe thereby creating a vacuum. The leading vehicle of the train was fixed to a piston within the pipe, and a linking arm slid in the slot, lifting the flap. Atmospheric pressure entered the pipe behind the piston and exerted up to a ton of force which propelled the train.

This system, which was also used on the London to Croydon line, had been rejected by the Stephensons. George said that it was little better than using rope haulage. Isambard, however, saw that light trains could be run at high speeds over gradients that caused trouble for steam locomotives. He recommended that the South Devon Railway should be a single line, atmospheric system. By September 1847, fifteen miles between Exeter and Teignmouth became operational, and in January 1848 the service reached Newton Abbot. However, despite the fact that an amazing 68 miles per hour had been recorded with a 28 ton train, the atmospheric experiment was discontinued later the same year.

It had been an expensive and embarrassing mistake which had cost the South Devon's shareholders several hundreds of thousands of pounds. Brunel himself had invested, and lost, his own money. Expensive Italianate pumping houses had been constructed with good quality steam pumping engines within them. Fuel costs had been high, and the constant attention to the continuous leather flap that was required in order to maintain an airtight seal had not been foreseen. After September 1848 the line was worked throughout by steam locomotives.

Brunel the Heroic Engineer

London was finally connected to Plymouth in April 1849, and the 249 mile journey which once took several days by stage coach could now be done in seven hours. In order to take the line over the slopes of Dartmoor, Isambard built a number of cheap timber viaducts of impressive height. His viaduct at Ivybridge had eleven 60 foot spans with a maximum height of 104 feet. The piers were of masonry and were quite slender. These timber bridges and viaducts were cleverly designed and carefully pre-tested to discover the loading limits of yellow pine. The most graceful of his bridges was probably the one built across the Thames at Maidenhead, where semi elliptical arches of

brick span a distance of 128 feet, very large for brickwork and much criticised at the time for being 'unsafe'. This bridge still serves the line today, now carrying far heavier trains than were originally anticipated.

Perhaps his most impressive bridge was the Royal Albert at Saltash. A bridge had to be provided over the Tamar River about three miles west of Plymouth in order to connect Plymouth with Penzance for the Cornwall Railway Company. Navigational requirements stipulated a hundred feet of mast room at high tide. The river at this point is just over a thousand feet wide. To keep the costs down, Brunel designed a single track bridge with an overall length of 2,200 feet. It had two main spans of 455 feet each and one central pier. Seventeen approach spans rest on masonry piers.

In 1853 work began on the central pier, the depth of water at high tide could be almost seventy feet. To create a 90 foot column of masonry Brunel floated an iron cylinder, which had been put together on the river bank, to the correct position before lowering it vertically onto the river bed. It took three and a half years to build the masonry foundations within the cylinder.

The two main spans, which weighed 1,000 tons each, were also constructed on the shore and tested under load. The first span was floated on pontoons into place between the piers in September 1857. Isambard directed operations from a platform erected in the centre of a truss, rather like a ship's bridge. It was to be a two hour session of intense concentration that probably reminded him of the occasion when, some years before, he had been at Robert Stephenson's side during the building of the Britannia Bridge. The span settled into position, a perfect fit, and was

slowly lifted by three foot increments until in July 1858 it was at its design height, 100 feet above the river at high tide. The second span was put in place under the directions of his assistant R P Brererton in July 1858. By then Isambard was a sick man and spent months abroad convalescing. He no longer signed the half yearly reports after August 1857. When the Royal Albert Bridge was formally opened by the Prince Consort in May 1859, Isambard was not present. Later that year, a terminally ill Brunel lay on a couch in a wagon while a special train hauled him across the bridge that had been so difficult to complete.

His final creation, the steamship Great Eastern, had been conceived while Isambard was in the early stages of designing this famous bridge. In fact, in 1853, when the central pier's foundations were under construction, tenders were being invited for the construction of the giant ship, which was to weigh almost 19,000 tons. The Eastern Steam Navigation Company, which was after the contract to convey mail to the far east, had accepted Isambard's design for a ship which he claimed would carry enough coal (10,000 tons) to make the return journey without refuelling. It would be three times the size of the Great Britain.

Shipbuilder John Scott Russell's tender had been accepted and his yard was on the north bank of the Thames at Millwall, Isle of Dogs. Unable to afford to make a dock of the size required, Russell's solution was to construct the hull parallel to the river bank 300 feet from the low water mark. This meant that the ship would have to be launched sideways. The 692 foot long hull was made from 30,000 one inch plates, 10 feet by 2 feet 9 inches, which formed a double skin 2 feet 10 inches apart. To drive her through the

water, Russell was to build the two great paddle wheels 53 feet in diameter, and the engines that would drive them. James Watt and Co. were contracted to build the engines that drove a 24 foot screw.

After four years of work on the muddy river bank, a launching date was set for the 3rd November 1857 (the first span of the Royal Albert Bridge at Tamar had just been put into place). In order to encourage the 12,000 ton hull to slide into the river without 'sticking', Isambard decided to install iron plates sliding on rails at a gradient of one in twelve resting on a timber and concrete platform. A great crowd gathered to watch. The steam winches on barges in the river pulled mightily and hydraulic rams were applied to the hull on the landward side. Despite two attempts the ship hardly budged and the crowd went home, disappointed.

A further attempt was made on the 30th November, when the ship moved thirty-three feet - and stuck again. Public interest was intense, and Isambard received advice from all and sundry. His friend, Robert Stephenson, provided moral support and some good advice as he attended the scene despite his own failing health. At last, on 31st January 1858, the Great Eastern was floated at high tide. No sooner was one problem solved than another arose, as the Eastern Steam Navigation Co. ran out of money. Scott Russell had been bankrupted, Brunel was working without salary - he had lost his investment too. The Great Ship Company was formed to complete the vessel. Isambard was now seriously ill and often abroad in search of healthier climes. He was unable to attend a banquet held after the engines were tested in the summer of 1859. He made his final visit to the ship on

Brunel the Heroic Engineer

2nd September, the day before she was due to make her maiden voyage to Holyhead. The photograph to which I refer at the opening of this chapter was taken that day. He stood unsupported for the picture to be taken, but soon collapsed and was rushed home to his sick bed at Great Duke Street.

On 8th September, while the Great Eastern was in the English Channel, one of the ship's funnels exploded. The huge water heater within it had become over pressured. Five stokers were killed and several others seriously injured. The terrible news reached Isambard on 10th September, and he died five days later. He was in his fifty-third year.

Isambard's life had been devoted to the advancement of a new means of transport that forever altered the way we regulate our clocks and our working lives. His fame does not result from the advancement of the steam locomotive, the locomotive designs that he had specified for the new Great Western Railway in 1836 had poor reputations and short lives. It was the young engineer, Daniel Gooch, who had learned his trade at Robert Stephenson's side who eventually provided the Great Western with efficient locomotives largely based on Stephenson's North Star 2-2-2. However, as the creator of the feat that was the Great Western Railway, and the magnificent steamships which transformed the navigation of the sea, I K Brunel is truly the engineer hero of this book of British Steam.

PREVIOUS PAGE
The steamship Great Eastern being constructed under the direction of Isambard Kingdom Brunel.

BELOW
The Great Eastern sets sail with the Atlantic telegraph cable on board. She is flying British and American flags, 1866.